AF479357

AT THE HEART OF IT ALL

# AT THE HEART
# OF IT ALL

## PETRI JUNTUNEN

HATJE
CANTZ

# FOREWORD

*Timothy Persons*

Petri Juntunen in his most recent publication *At The Heart of it All* visually explores the question of how to measure the volume of existence. However existential this might seem initially, Juntunen's interpretation of it ranges from stones to places seemingly forgotten, using light and shades of darkness as a means to capture the history of their passing. Having spent most of my adult life in Finland, I found Juntunen's choice of light to build a bridge between past and present quite natural. The Nordic region in general fine-tunes your senses to the ever-changing seasons; whether you like it or not, it's a part of your daily life. Finding that internal balance between the solstices and equinoxes plays an important role in the Nordic psyche. Juntunen's photographs are not about the object itself but the process of perception and how he leads us to experience it. His choice of places can be anywhere. He stages the non-specific and uses it to create stories without endings, interludes that introduce what was to what can be. His images, stripped down to their material essence, encapsulate a feeling of time standing still. The photographs, with their velvet-like aura, emerge from a shrouded darkness and become time capsules marked with the patterns of their ageless passage. His world is one that stands stoically silent, invoking shadowless memories that are sometimes heavier then the foundations they are built upon. Nevertheless, as a whole these pictures work as peepholes into another frame of mind, binding the viewer to a presence stronger than faith, illuminating a voluminous echo of the here and now.

# INTIMATE DISCLOSURE

The Photography of Petri Juntunen

*Mark Gisbourne*

The most singular aspect of photography is that of disclosure in the way it reveals an assertion of an existent aspect of phenomenal presence. It evokes the sense of a once and current "thingness" in the world, and this remains a constant, regardless of any later occasioned editorial interventions. For—unlike the ever-varying temporal processes of painting that depart into a world that is selectively and materially imagined, the optical speculative, an interpretative moment of visual projection—the photograph always attests to an existent reality of intimate disclosure. This prevails notwithstanding issues that operate today around virtual images, for the cognitive reality of the photographic image is that it invariably refers to an original "thingly" aspect, something that the photographer has excised from the being world. This nature of material presence and existential disclosure, a sense of the strangely familiar or uncanny, the "un-concealing" of things, is of primary concern and continued assimilation in the photography practice of the Finnish artist-photographer Petri Juntunen.[1] Yet his powerful appropriation of the Heideggerian sense of *aletheia* (the state of being evident) has less to do with the conventional truth of an image than with, the preparative state of apprehension as to how the thing looked at is able to appear as a sensory entity of some consequence in the world.[2] In other words, how the world discloses itself through an "opening" (one might argue an aperture) that gives sense to the feeling of a strangely familiar ("adequatio") certitude. We know that photographs taken of the world are nothing more than reproductive images, representative acknowledgements of entities and existent thingness (Heidegger denies the "a priori" subject-object relations of traditional aesthetics), but at the same time they represent how the ontological status of the world is disclosed and opened up.[3] It is through this process that we gain access to the intuitive and the strangely familiar contents of a photograph. That is to say, access to the defining constituents of the "punctum" and "studium" of photographic images.[4]

The artist's "strangely familiar" (to quote Heidegger) contents of a photograph, sometimes referred to as *unheimlich*, or uncanny, are best understood via an immediate example by Juntunen, whose images are imbued with a powerful preternatural sense of mystery.[5] For an anxious state of puzzlement is an essential characteristic of the uncanny, a flickering sense of disequilibrium and a feeling that one is disturbed as to who one is and what is actually being experienced. The photograph entitled *The Ship Called Night* is a case in point: it shows an anonymous boat drawn up on a beach and seemingly abandoned, its eerie presence a spectral promissory of uncertainty and psychological otherness. Powerfully focused and strategically lit by the artist-photographer, it evokes a sense that goes far beyond the immediacy of its mere "thingly" presence and the expressive literary allusion that its chosen title initially provides.[6] The image represents a wider if uncertain state of disclosure and is perversely Romantic, to the extent that it breaches states of the repressed, as do all experiences that are said to be uncanny. Romantic, that is to say, in the modality of the philosopher Friedrich Schelling's thought, who was, perhaps, the first to observe that the Western origins of literary, and by extension representative visual, clarity were built upon an *a priori* repression of uncanny impulses.[7] In consequence we can speak of the strangely familiar or evocative contents of this image as working through uncertain disclosed psychological counter-affects, and these affective contents are made distinct from a state of immediate narrative clarity. Thus an image such as *The Ship Called Night* operates in an interstitial space (an existential space) between darkness and light, what in earlier aesthetics were considered as Romantically derived and aesthetically motivated uses of diurnal transitions.[8] The sailboat in question was found abandoned by Juntunen on the coastline

east of Helsinki, and the artist photographically acknowledges its sense of existential presence that becomes an appropriate reason for its staged presentation. The theme of darkness and light as the symbolic transitions of night are therefore central to the series of photographic works here represented. But it is equally important to stress that when we speak of photographic "staging" it has little to do with purposive artificiality, and we are more concerned with the implicit *uncanniness* or *eidolon* of a photograph, "that rather terrible thing which is there in every photograph: the return of the dead." [9] These eschatological fantasies as to various apocalyptic viewpoints, mortality myths, and human cravings for continuity are integral to this current series of photographs.[10] Juntunen is committed to investigations into Western eschatological culture and is currently researching its extensive literature.[11]

The nature of darkness and death are always associated with the night both intellectually and spiritually, since theologically speaking the diurnal round bears temporal witness to life, death, and to a metaphorical spiritual resurrection renewed each day.[12] Yet a photograph like *Announcement of Absence*, which depicts a military graveyard, while not intended explicitly as a religious image by this artist-photographer, nonetheless evokes a powerful and purposive transcendent state of self-intuited temporality. It is a photograph of a First World War graveyard of Italian soldiers, the responsibility for which was contested for many years between Italy and Slovenia (when it was part of Yugoslavia), making the artist's chosen title somewhat paradoxical and perhaps intended as a visual irony of inversion—as absent presence through symbolic disclosure.[13] More significantly still, a focused finger of light rakes a sharp horizontal incision left to right across the centre field of the image of gravestones, echoing a second and intense level of feeling and a further wound to the long interred remains and the once contested bodies. For questions of absence and presence are of paramount concern in many of these Juntunen images, since such images touch upon existential allusions to the concealed and the unconcealed. At the same time the idea and use of painter-like tenebrism exposes an incised wound, demarcated through the use of striated light that appears in a number of the images; for example, *A Sense of Foreboding* and *The Passage (Erebus)*. The images function surprisingly by using both denotative and connotative terms of reference: that is, as literal descriptive indexes as well as having extended and inferred symbolic meanings. In consequence *A Sense of Foreboding* is a somewhat ominous quarry-like image of an illuminated trench, creating a sense that might hint at an anonymous action of interment or disinterment, since matters are left open and eerily unresolved. *The Passage (Erebus)* and accompanying *The Passage (Terror)* are illuminated night-time seascapes that refer to the last and fatal Franklin Expedition, whose ships and crews were lost while searching for the elusive North West passage in the mid-nineteenth century.[14] At the same time the former image encompasses in its title the darkness of Erebus: an allusion to the transitional darkness of the mythological underworld (the world of the dead), and, perhaps, also to sadness at the ill fate of the ships brutally crushed in the ice.[15] The eschatological or sense of an absent presence is also made evident in images entitled *Apeiron* taken by the artist while on a visit to the Camargue. These are again dramatically lit night images, but of abandoned enclosures, perhaps pens once used for various domesticated animals on the beach (goats, chickens, geese, etc.). The flimsy fragility of these now derelict structures again echoes the use of the indexical *vis-à-vis* the symbolic nature of the image, as the Greek term *apeiron* actually refers to that which is considered unlimited or boundless.[16] Hence the idea and use of psychical contraries—endings and endlessness, finitude and the eternal, the continuous and discontinuous, or epilogue and denouement—are considered as investigations that remain central to pictorial-cognitive researches made by the artist.[17]

It is self-evident Juntunen's existential contestation of subject-object, and his post-narrative approach to creative image-making through photography, expresses and emphasizes an abstracted state of thingness that is closely allied to sensory forms of a being presence. His work is a denial of the passive and schismatically forced aesthetic separation between the subjective self (the viewer viewing) and exterior objects (that which is looked at), and this in turn reinforces the artist's interpretative ambitions and greater existential aims. It is made explicit in photographs like *Aletheia* and *Where I End and You Begin*. What is revealed in *Aletheia* is that which was once concealed and is now seen in the visual process of unfolding, in a transitional state of becoming evident. At the same time *Where I End and You Begin* intimates a creative and intended state of mutual synthesis between self and other, a phenomenological entity against which visual and individual personal identities are constructed and subsequently become real. Hence the self and other come together in the vaporous cascade that falls and fuses in its passage, flowing through a sylvan organic-vulva and expressively suggesting those greater earthbound forces within chthonic nature. The chthonic is a material allusion to that which is subterranean, the mythic underworld and hiddenness of things ever awaiting their eventual "un-concealment."[18] A Heideggerian existential approach to contemporary aesthetics thus denies the forced separation of the subject and object. It rejects *a priori* privilege as to a separate state of subjective being, since we are foremost and already, as Heidegger argues, pre-immersed within the *Dasein* of lived existence in the world.[19] As regards these photographs, the use of particular geographical locations and relevant sources is various: Iceland, Finland, France Italy, Poland, among others. But this should have no immediate significance for the viewer, as the images are intentionally made to be non-topographical, and we might learn little beyond the ordinary visual-indexical referent to a location unless we already knew it. For example *Gardenia*, or *House of Lilith*, and *Katabasis* tell us little that is specific to the place photographed save in the most generalized of visual terms. Yet what they do reveal is highly emotive at another, far deeper level, partly due to the fact that they are evocations of mental projection and later discovery. They accord as discoveries that were in some respects in waiting, following on from the many drawings and sometimes even painted thoughts that we find in the artist's preliminary notes and drawings and which form the basis of the execution of later photographs. An image such as *Gardenia* is extraordinary, with its centralized pool of light and painterly composition. While the natural environment photographed has

loose echoes of an Italian or Provencal origin, it might be seen just as readily as a metaphor or topological essence that we simply associate with the embodied pictorial garden and horticultural conventions of southern Europe. And this is doubly so, as *Gardenia* compositionally affirms, through visual reminiscence: the background of Renaissance paintings like Leonardo's famous *Annunciation* (1472). *The House of Lilith* is similar; it may derive, as the artist has intimated, from an empty ruin in southern France, yet it says more about the memorial and literary evocations of its title than the actual source of the environment photographed. Lilith, after all, was a mythical female demon of the night familiar to ancient Jewish Talmudic folklore, and to pseudo-biblical inclusion.[20] In this context Lilith more likely emphasizes the preternatural embodiment of the sensory erotic(s) of nature as aspects fundamental to understanding phenomenological-existentialism—the body is always materially in the world.[21] The corollary is the image *Katabasis*, also suggestive of an embodied source, the wellspring of human phenomenological existence, expressed rhetorically as a metaphorical inner descent and psychical journey into the underworld.[22]

Issues of memory and the trace form another vital component to be considered in Juntunen's night-time series of photographs. When asked why the lighting has in each instance such a tightly confined focus, the artist explains that he needs it for technical as well as emotive reasons, otherwise the contents of the image "bleed out," and the internal sense of emotional pressure becomes lost. He speaks of the yearning and longing aspects of his images, and, as with his frequent use of bilateral symmetry, of the distilled intensities of human feelings as analogous in his mind with those found in the structures of literature.[23] Yet the distinction is that the images are not related to temporality and/or intended as narrative storytelling but about ontological presence. A watchtower from Auschwitz, as in *Routine of a Broken Machine*, or the flooded and isolated tower of a church in *Abandonment of Being* carry the traces of history and interrogative states of betrayal. The visual centrality of the main motif in these images gives them a sense of totemic accusation; in the former that of the holocaust atrocities of the National Socialist regime, and in the latter that of flooding and enforced village abandonment in 1950.[24] In fact the deferred symbolic nature of each of the two towers is reinforced by the pathetic effect, paradoxically suborned by the chosen titles, of former human life and existential presence ("being") subsequently abandoned. Yet, strangely, traces of the human are everywhere in these sequestered images, all the more present for their obvious absence. In photographs such as *Cinders There Are*, or the images *Outlines of Fractures* and *The History of This World and the Other*, human presence is manifested through notions of the palimpsest or trace.[25] Here the status of existent being is made residual through opaque, allusive states of indexical transcription, for the trace is a mark of the absence of a presence cognizant to thought and experience. *Cinders There Are* is a detailed image of the wall from an Auschwitz gas chamber; similarly, *Outlines of Fractures* attests to scarified surfaces ruptured by pre-existing human intervention. Yet in *The History of This World and Other*, which pairs the shared ontology of being in the world with the speculative and extended "other", alterity is expressed through the detail of a sweeping fan-like gesture and an imaginary umbilical thread. The artist has acknowledged memory in conversation with the present author: "I also work through the past and remembering." The trace is inevitably a memorial, for it not only convokes or summons up that which is associative but also opens up access to the hidden essential nature of a formerly complete entity. To put it another way, it makes it instrumental, as in so-called *A Borrowed State of Being*, following Heidegger's idea that existential disclosure affords to an entity an authentic position of consequence in the world. In the same way, the moss-covered rocks in *Only the Sound Remains* takes on a curious significance far greater than the commonplace banality of the image and its apparent contents. Memory and the trace are a consequential aftermath, and, like all the images in the present edition, connote the quantitative death that is exposed by photography. This gives a further plaintive power to *Letters of Last Resort*, an image of dead and frozen sunflowers; flowers pregnant with historical painterly associations that follow the solar determiner of our diurnal planetary existence referred to as the daily round. In *Lamentations* a Tolkienesque tree dramatically emerges from the hidden gloom of night, its trunk hollowed out as if baring its bowels to the world. For night time is synonymous with passage, as it is with death and lamentation, "arise, cry out in the night," [26] and this arboreal sentinel stands as a silent witness to the powerful poetics of Petri Juntunen's images of intimate disclosure.

ENDNOTES

1    Martin Heidegger's appropriation of the Greek *aletheia*, meaning "disclosure" (*Erschlossenheit*), that is "unclosedness" or "unconcealedness," first appeared in his major work *Being and Time* (*Sein und Zeit,* 1927), and as "world disclosure" constitutes that which is already known and interpreted in the world, and at a another level the "previously hidden or unthematized dimensions of present and future meaning;" see Hubert Dreyfus and Charles Spinosa, "Further Reflections on Heidegger, Technology and the Everyday," in Nikolas Kompridis (ed.), *Philosophical Romanticism* (New York, 2006), pp. 265–81.

2    This forms Heidegger's interpretative distinction of the Classical Greek use of *aletheia*, since it has less to do with the condition of truth than with how things first appear as disclosed entities. "To raise the question of *aletheia*, of disclosure as such, is not the same as raising the question of truth. For this reason, it was inadequate and misleading to call aletheia, in the sense of opening, truth"; Martin Heidegger, "The End of Philosophy and the Task of Thinking," *On Time and Being*, trans. John Stambaugh (London, [1972] 1977), pp. 55–73 (p. 70).

3    This is discussed exegetically in Julian Young, "The Origin of a Work of Art," *Heidegger's Philosophy of Art* (Cambridge, 2001) pp. 5–68 (this chapter should not be confused with the essay of the same title written by Martin Heidegger between 1935 and 1937, though it interprets it).

4    Roland Barthes, *Camera Lucida: Reflections on Photography* (London, 1984) (French original, *La chambre claire: note sur la photographie*, Paris, 1980).

The *studium* is the subject matter as contents, that either are of interest to the viewer, "the order is of the order of liking not of loving; it mobilizes a half-desire, a demi-volition," hence "the studium is clear, I am sympathetically interested, as a docile cultural subject," whereas "the second element which will disturb the studium I shall there call punctum … A photograph's *punctum* is that accident which pricks me (but also bruises me), is poignant to me," and in consequence, though it is co-present with the *studium* in the image there is no way to verify a causal link, for if the *studium* utters visual responsibility "the *punctum* shows no preference for morality or good taste: the *punctum* can be ill-bred" (pp. 27, 43). This psychical or visual dichotomy appears vindicated and is fundamental to the reading of a photograph.

5    For an extended contemporary overview of the "uncanny", see Nicholas Royle, *The Uncanny* (Manchester and New York, 2003).

6    In a recorded conversation with the present author (Berlin, 3 June, 2017), the artist-photographer Juntunen made reference to Marguerite Duras as a possible literary inspiration. Yet a Heideggerian approach would concentrate rather on its phenomenological description, how it manifests itself as living experience in its abandoned state, going beyond correspondence theory (as a historical object with formal properties and made of matter) into the greater nexus of ship-beach-abandonment. In other words how the image "unconceals" itself to a viewing consciousness. See Martin Heidegger, "The Origin of a Work of Art," *Basic Writings*, trans. David Farrell Krell (New York, 2008), pp. 143–212 (German original, *Der Ursprung des Kunstwerkes*, Stuttgart, 1960).

7    The idea first emerges in Schelling's lectures on *Philosophie der Mythologie* (from 1835), and his definition of the uncanny is of something which ought to have been kept concealed but which has nevertheless come to light. Cited in Anthony Vidler, *The Architectural Uncanny: Essays in the Modern Unhomely* (Cambridge MA and London, 1994, p. 26). Schelling's subsequent influence on Sigmund Freud's psychoanalytic theory of the 'uncanny' thus becomes something self-evident.

8    The question of darkness is central to Freud's analysis of the "uncanny" as that "concealed, or kept from sight" and to the opaque status of the concept in general, see Royle, "Darkness", *The Uncanny, op cit.*, pp. 108–11.

9    Roland Barthes, *Camera Lucida op cit.*, p. 9; also cited in Royle, "Film" *The Uncanny, op cit.*, p.75.

10    Gustave Doré's famous illustrations to the Bible are an acknowledged influence, the images can be seen online at https://www.gutenberg.org/files/8710/8710-h/8710-h.htm (accessed 15 July 2017).

11    See Philippe Ariès, *The Hour of Our Death. The Classic History of Western Attitudes Toward Death Over the Last One Thousand Years,* trans. Helen Weaver. (New York, 1981, and London, 1982): originally a short study version as *Western Attitudes Toward Death*, trans. Patricia Ranum (Baltimore, 1975); *Essais sur l'histoire de la mort en Occident: du Moyen Âge à nos jours* (Paris, 1975).

12    Hence the canonical office concludes the day with the Song of Simeon *Nunc Dimittis* (Lord now lettest thou thy servant go in peace), and begins the day with the Song of Zechariah *Benedictus* (Blessed

be the Lord God of Israel), the night being that of passage from life to death and spiritual rebirth each day.

13    For graveyards invariably reveal the paradoxical relationship between the concealed and the unconcealed, and "irony" is such as to give a particular insight into Juntunen's Nordic photography, see Søren Kierkegaard, *Om Begrebet Ironi med stadigt Hensyn til Socrates* (*On the Concept of Irony with Continual Reference to Socrates* (Copenhagen, 1841). The work was Kierkegaard's doctoral thesis, which examined both classical and the then newly emerging Romantic theories of irony.

14    Scott Cookman, *Iceblink: The Tragic Fate of Sir John Franklin's Lost Polar Expedition* (New York, 2000). A general reference to Caspar David Friedrich and his famous 1823-4 painting *Sea of Ice (or The Wreck of Hope)* is immediately apparent.

15    Some remnants and artefacts from HMS *Erebus*, including the ship's bell, were found as recently as 2014; http://www.cbc.ca/news/canada/north/hms-erebus-ship-s-bell-recovered-from-franklin-expedition-1.2826455 (accessed 15 July 2017). In 2016 the second lost ship, HMS *Terror*, was discovered sunk in Terror Bay, south-west of King William Island.

16    The term was adopted and used by Anaximander (ca. 610-546 BCE) and became the basis for his cosmological theories; he believed that the beginnings or that which constituted ultimate reality is eternal and infinite, see Charles H. Kahn, *Anaximander and the Origins of Greek Cosmology* (New York,1960).

17    His current investigations follow closely the British literary critic Frank Kermode's *The Sense of An Ending: Studies in the Theory of Fiction* ([1967], Oxford, 2000).

18    The term "chthonic" is commonly used in Analytic Psychology to describe the spirit of nature within, the unconscious earthly impulses of the Self, one's material depths, without necessarily implying negative connotations. See Carl Gustav Jung, *Man and His Symbols* (London and New York, 1968) and all subsequent editions).

19    Heidegger's use of the term *Dasein* (being there) constituted an authentic existential immersion in the immediate world of the everyday, and the contingent yet evolving nature of the self in that context. For precise statements of definition for *Da-sein* see Martin Heidegger, *Being and Time*, trans. John Macquarrie and Edward Robinson, (Oxford, 1962), pp. 28-5, 67-90, and subsequent editions.

20    In Hebrew the etymology of the word Lilith is that of "night," deriving ultimately perhaps from an ancient Akkadian concept *Lilu* (spirit or demon), and appears in the earliest known work of literature *The Epic of Gilgamesh* (ca. 2100 BC). See Siegmund Hurwitz, *Lilith—The First Eve: Historical and Psychological Aspects of the Dark Feminine*, 2nd rev. ed. (Einsiedeln, 1999).

21    Maurice Merleau-Ponty, *The Visible and the Invisible*, trans. Alphonso Lingis, Evanston IL and London, 1968), p. 271 "the body *stands* before the world and the world upright before it, and between them there is a relation that is one of embrace. And between these two vertical beings, there is not a frontier but a contact surface." (French original *Le visible et l'invisible*, Paris, 1964.)

22    Orpheus's descent into the underworld is one example of a journey of *katabasis*, and numerous ancient myths, legends and theologies are full of such indicative journeys (e.g., Homer, Virgil, Ovid, or the biblical Jesus in the narrative of the Harrowing of Hell). See John J. Collins and Michael Fishbane (eds.) *Death, Ecstasy, and Other Worldly Journeys* (Albany, NY 1995).

23    The use of the term "structure of feeling" is associated with the literary scholar and novelist Raymond Williams. See the entry in Michael Payne (ed.), *Dictionary of Cultural and Critical Theory* (London and New York, 2009).

24    The image of the remaining Church Tower emerging from the water is from the village of Graun im Vinschgau (Curon Venosta) in the Italian South Tyrol, which was submerged in the Reschensee (Lago di Resia) reservoir in July 1950 (the hydro-electric dam was begun in 1940); see http://mentalfloss.com/article/20657/italys-most-famous-drowned-town (accessed 15 July 2017).

25    For the role of the trace in contemporary thought and its impact on deconstruction, see David Mikics, *Who Was Jacques Derrida? An Intellectual Biography* (London and New Haven CT, 2009), p. 91.

26    Lamentations 2:19 AV.

I

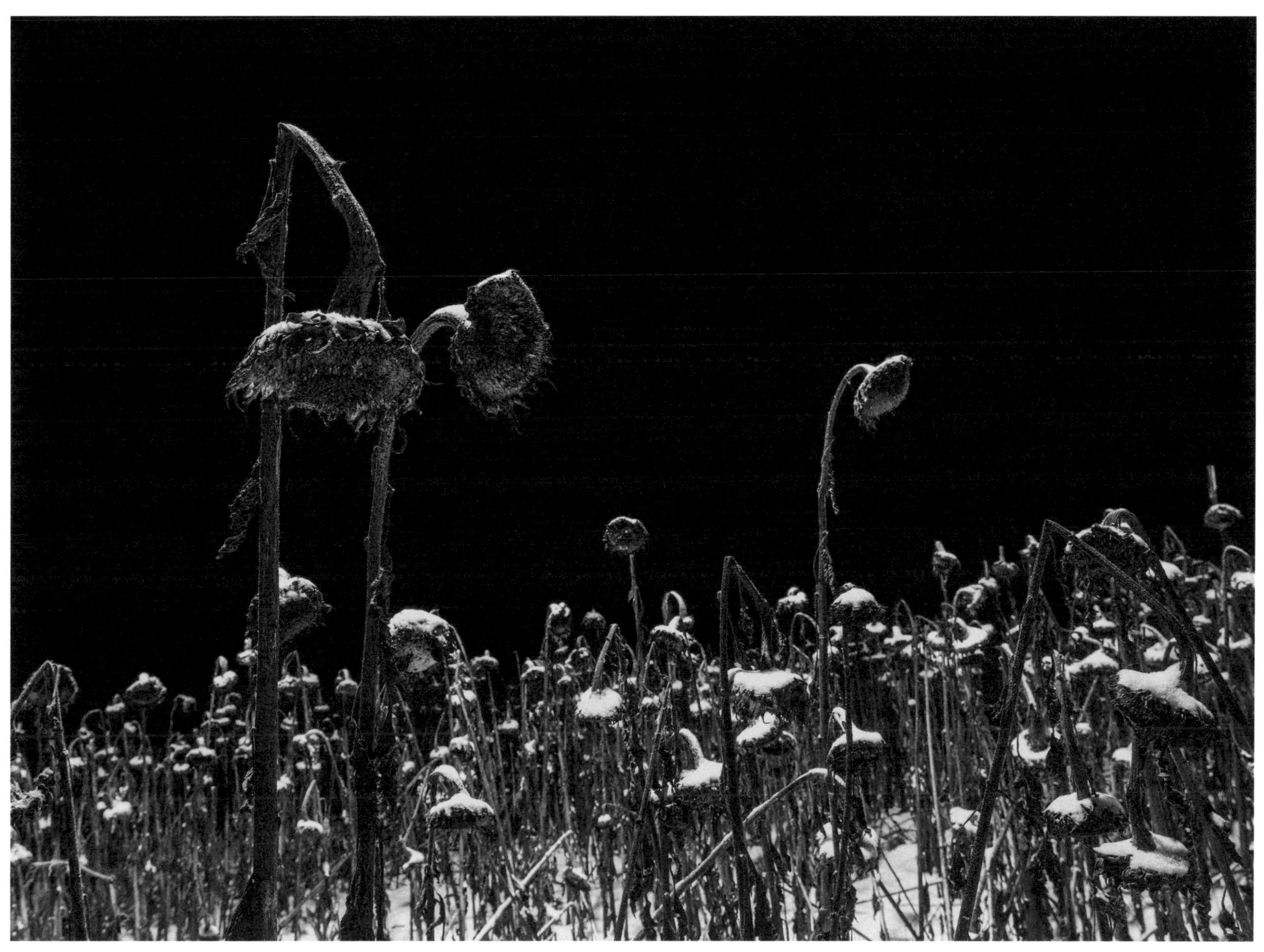

18

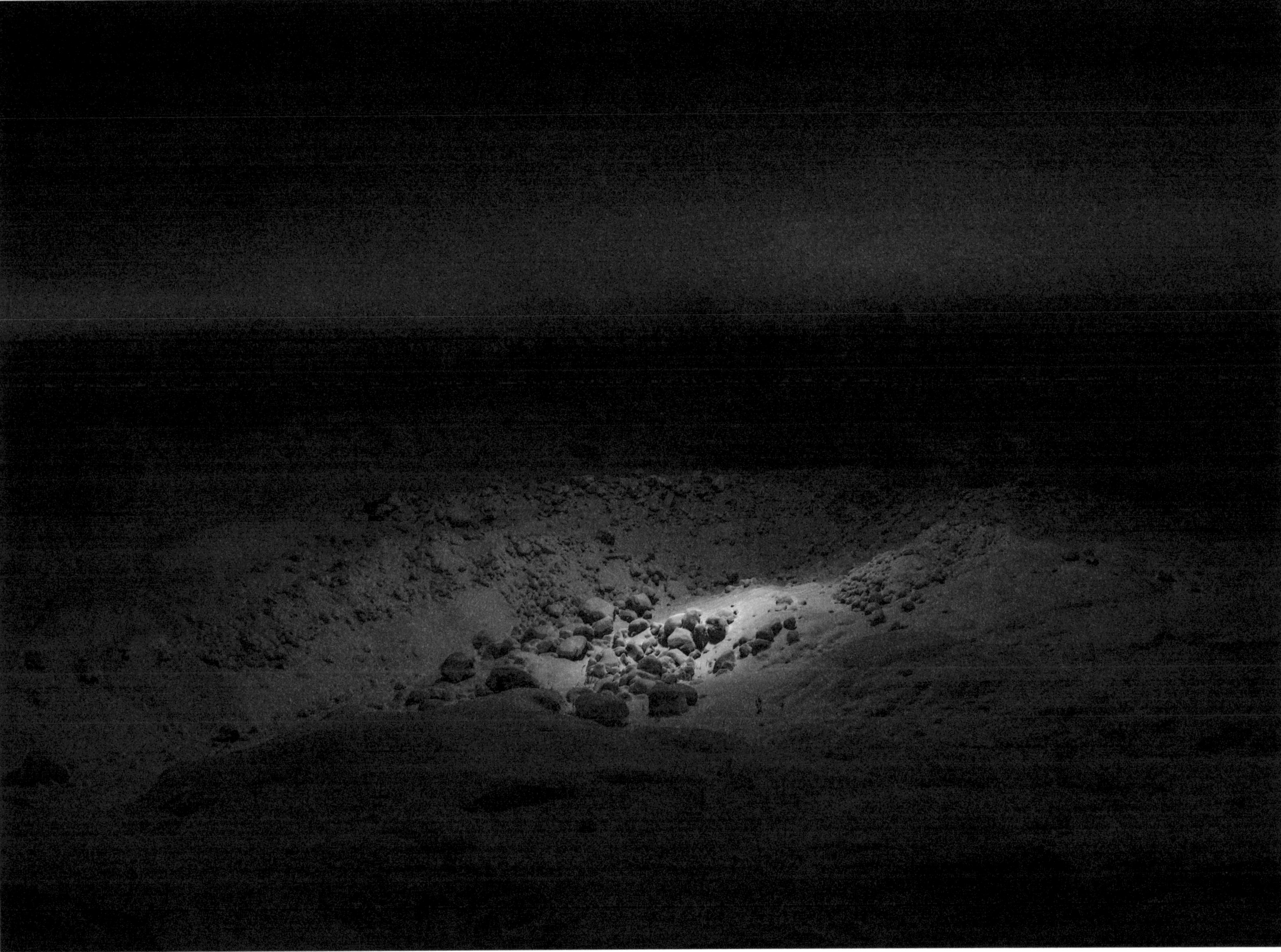

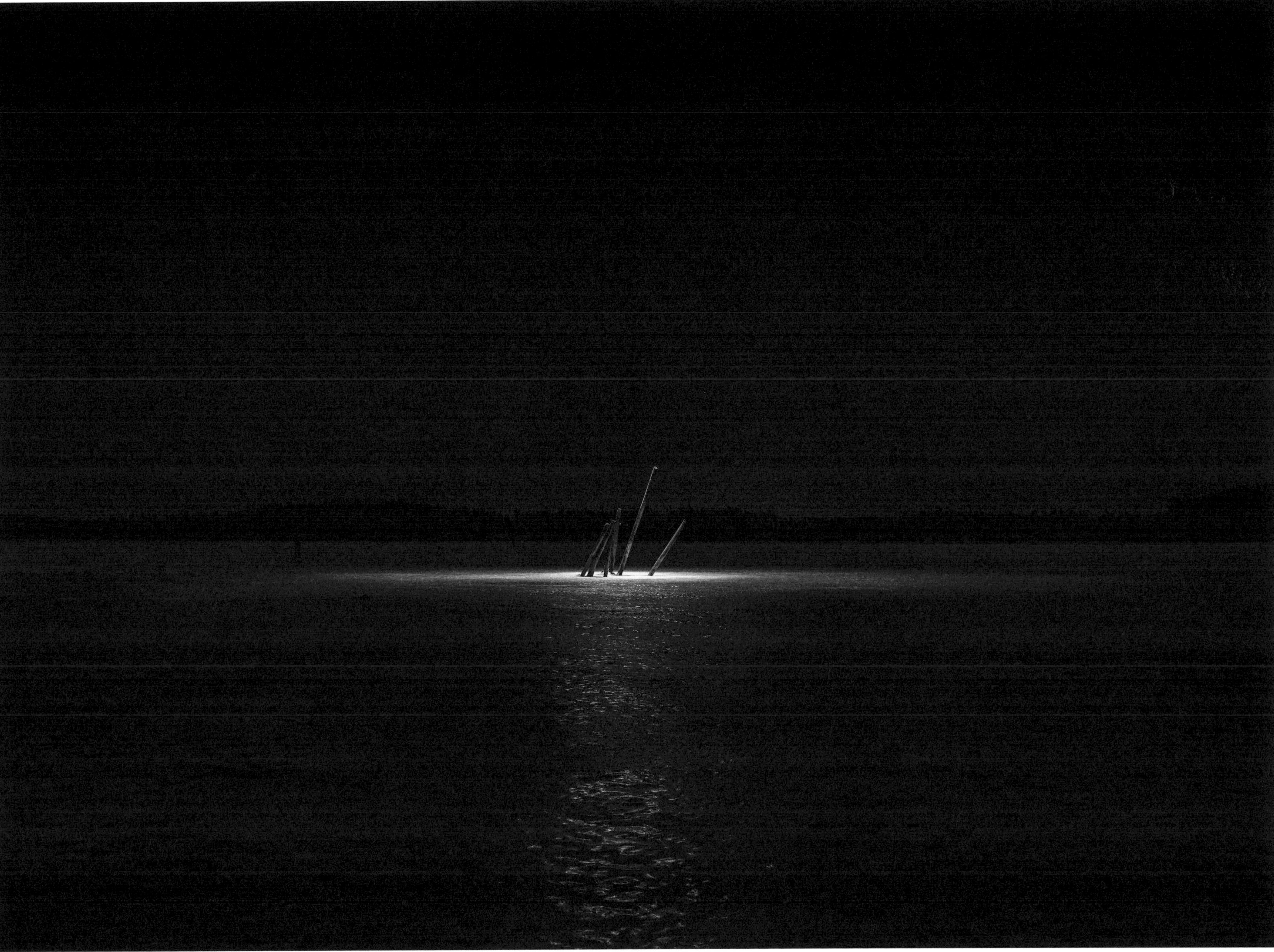

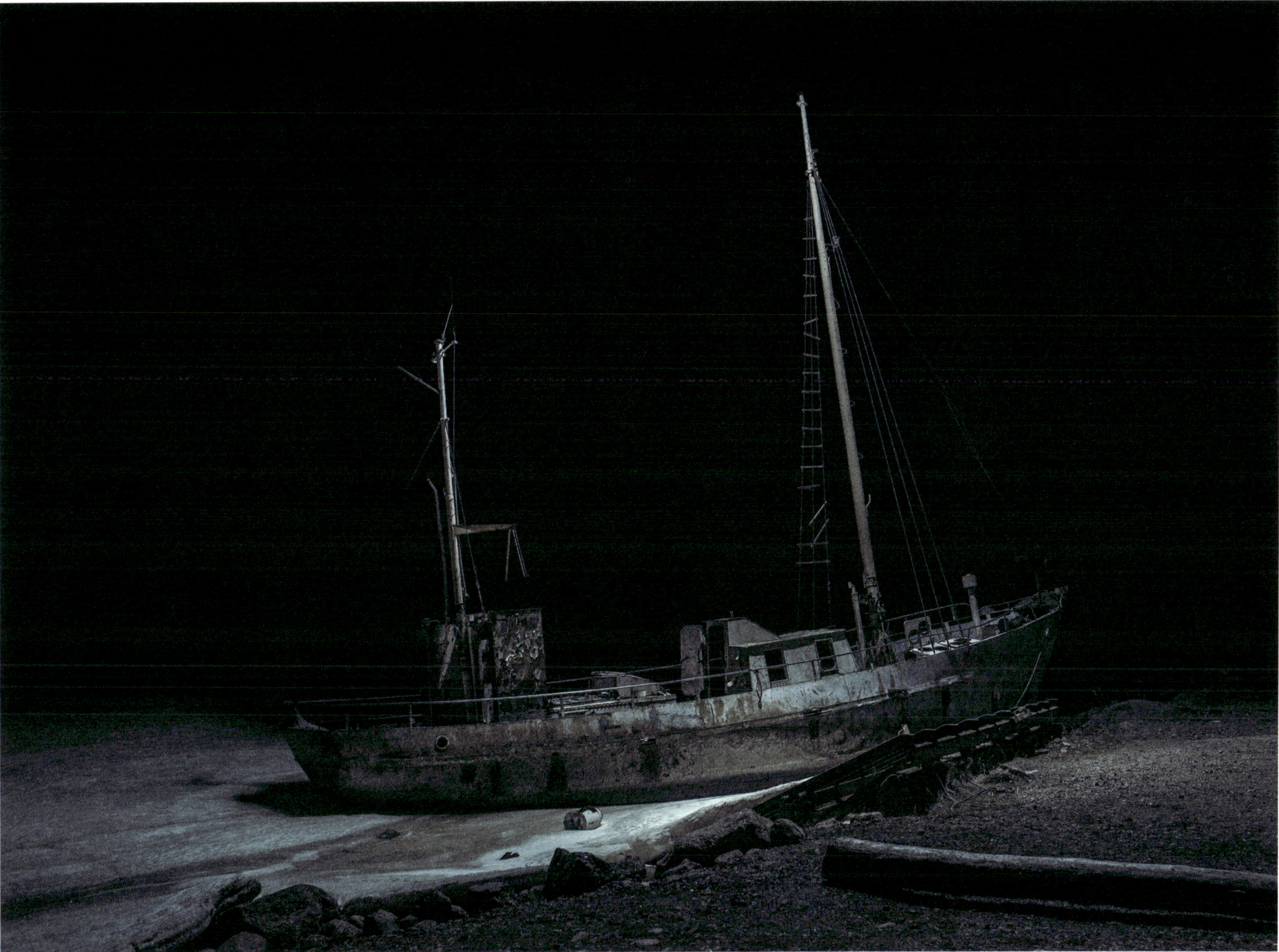

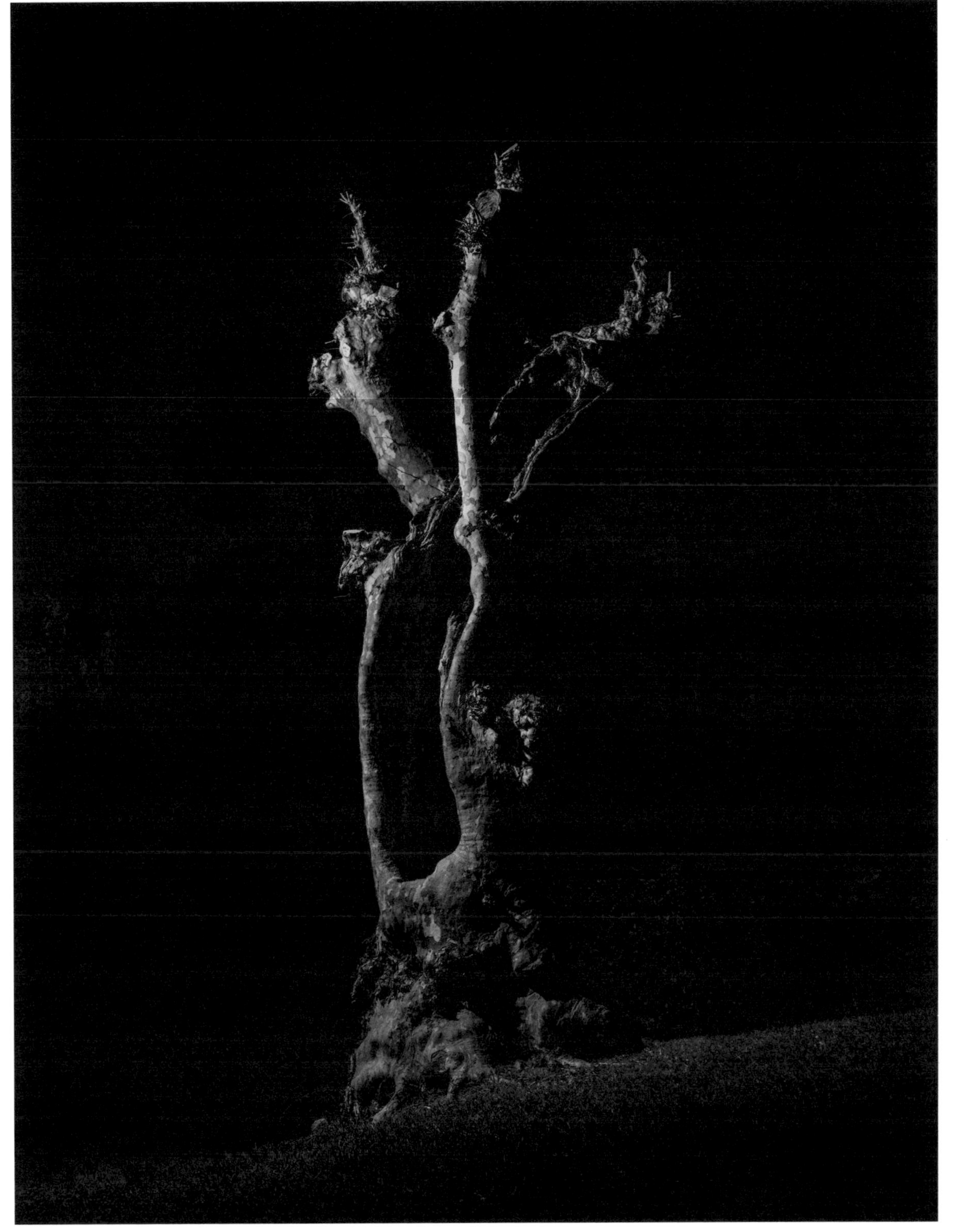

II

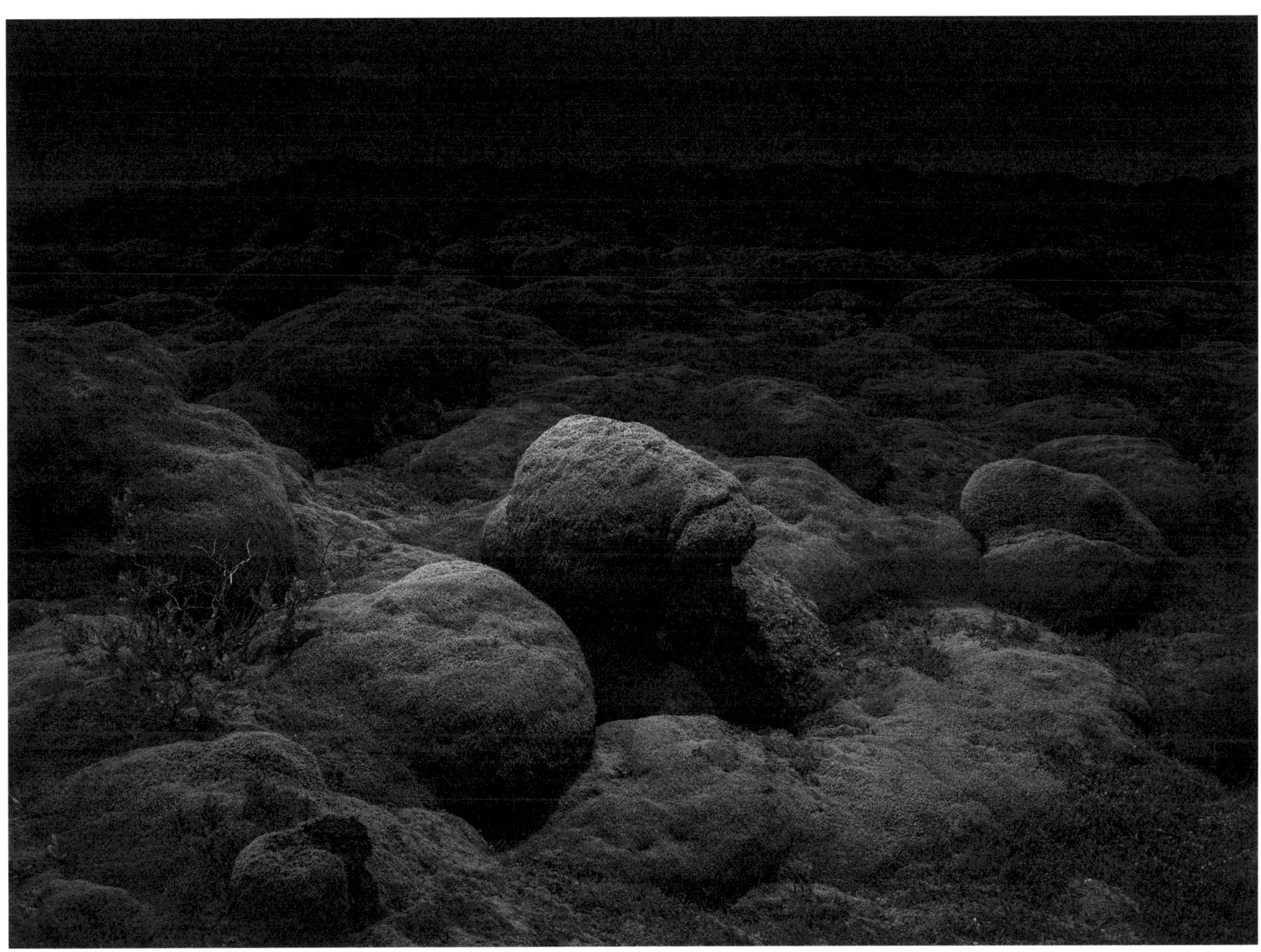

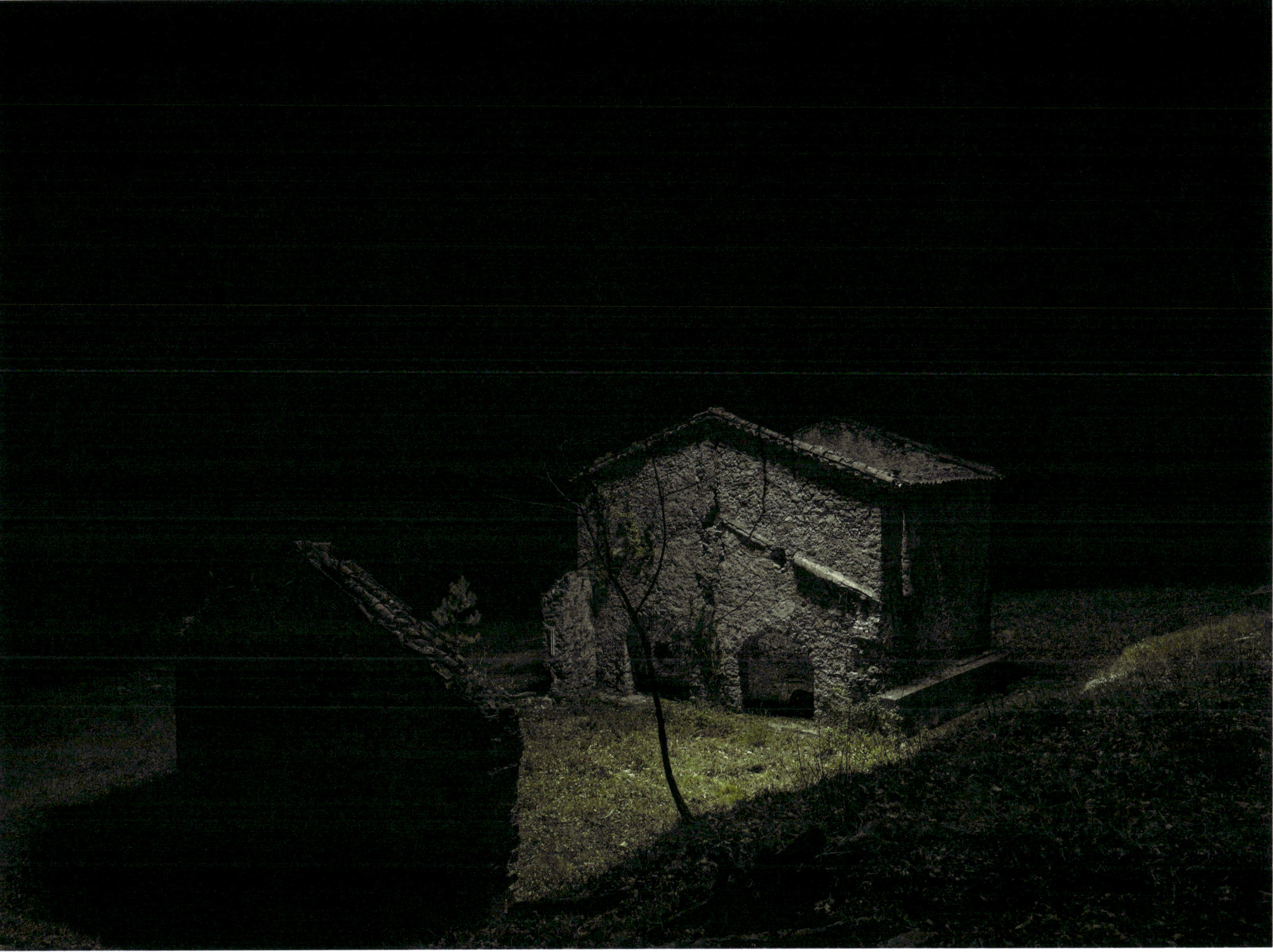

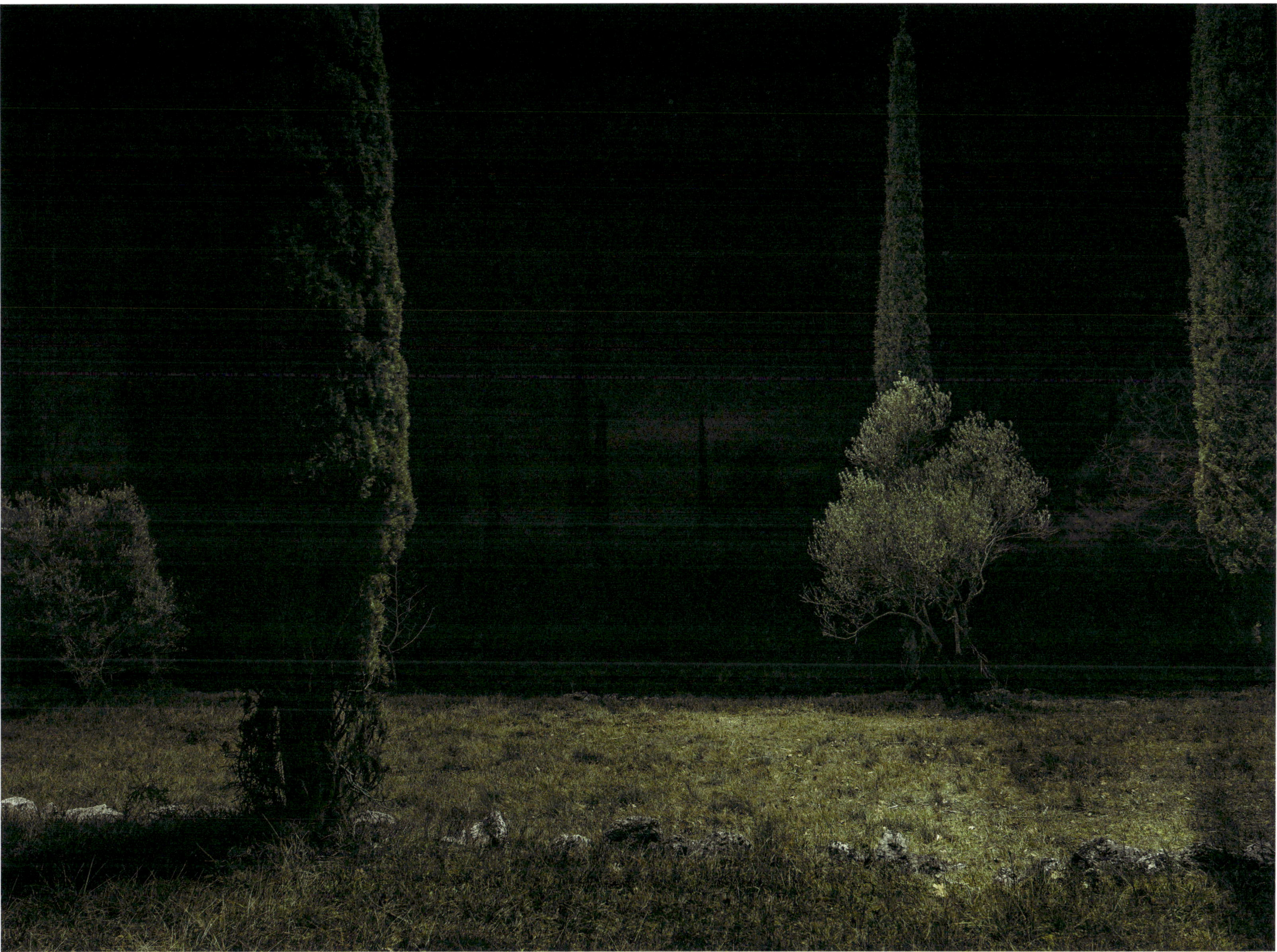

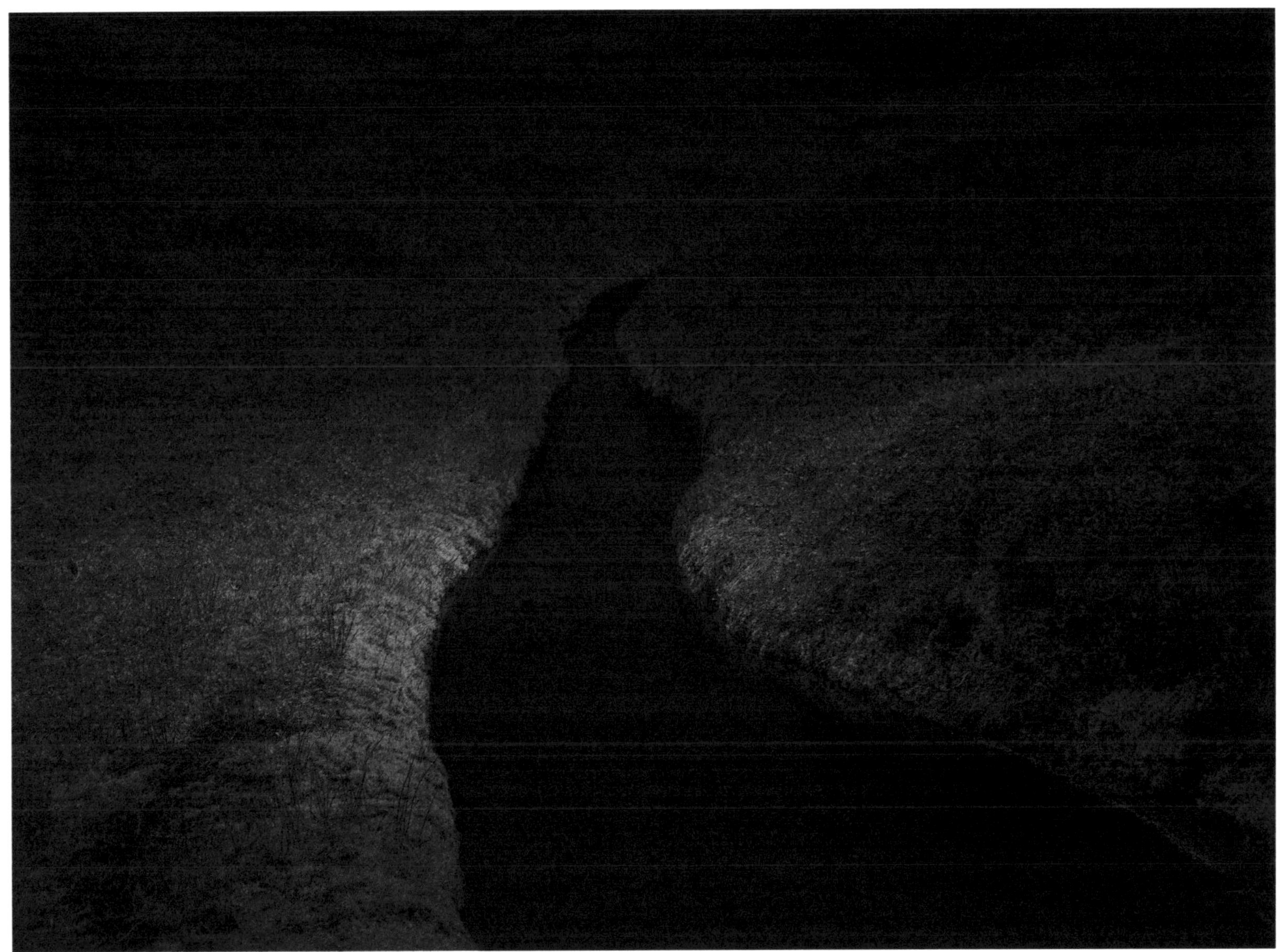

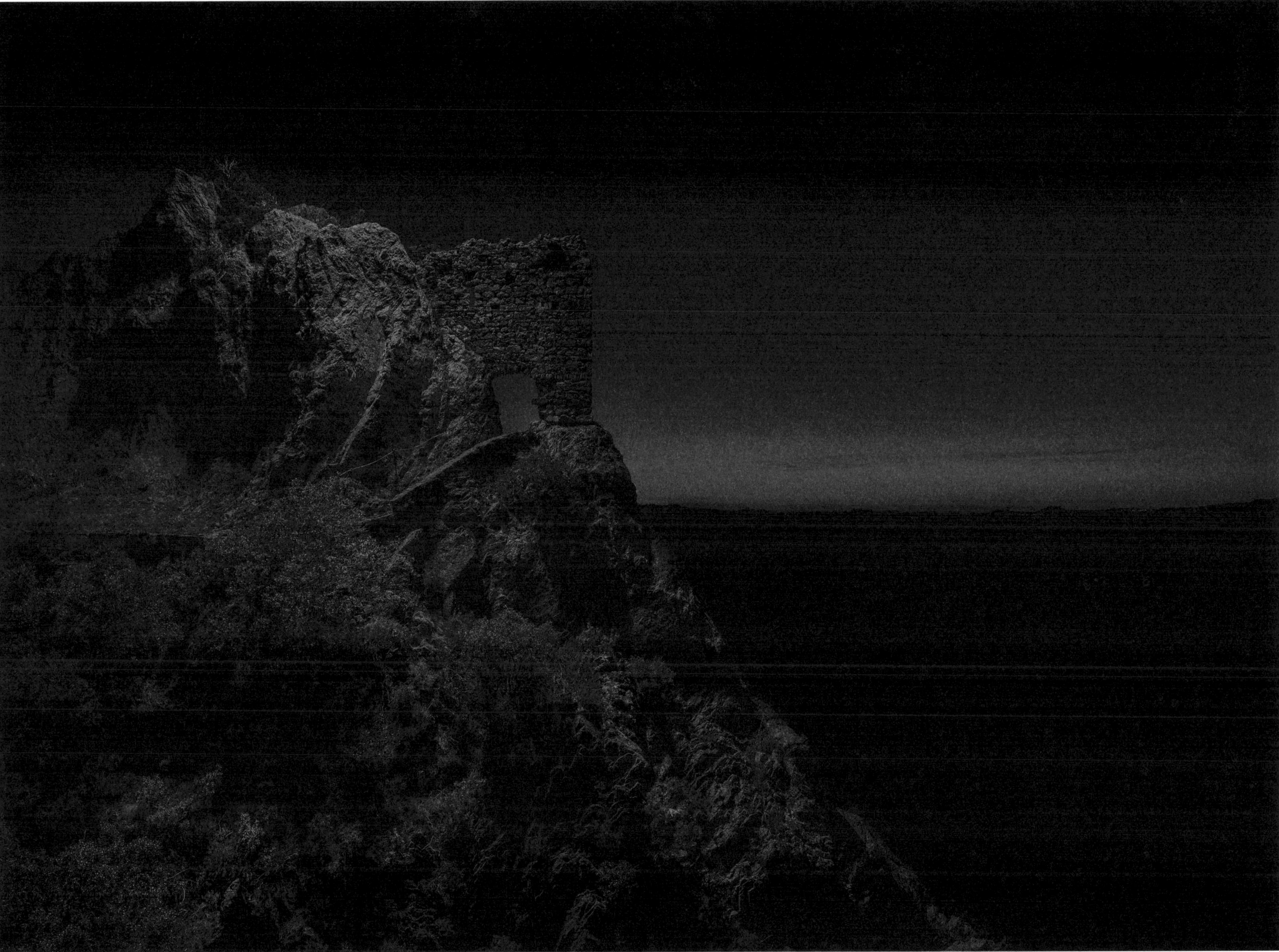

# III

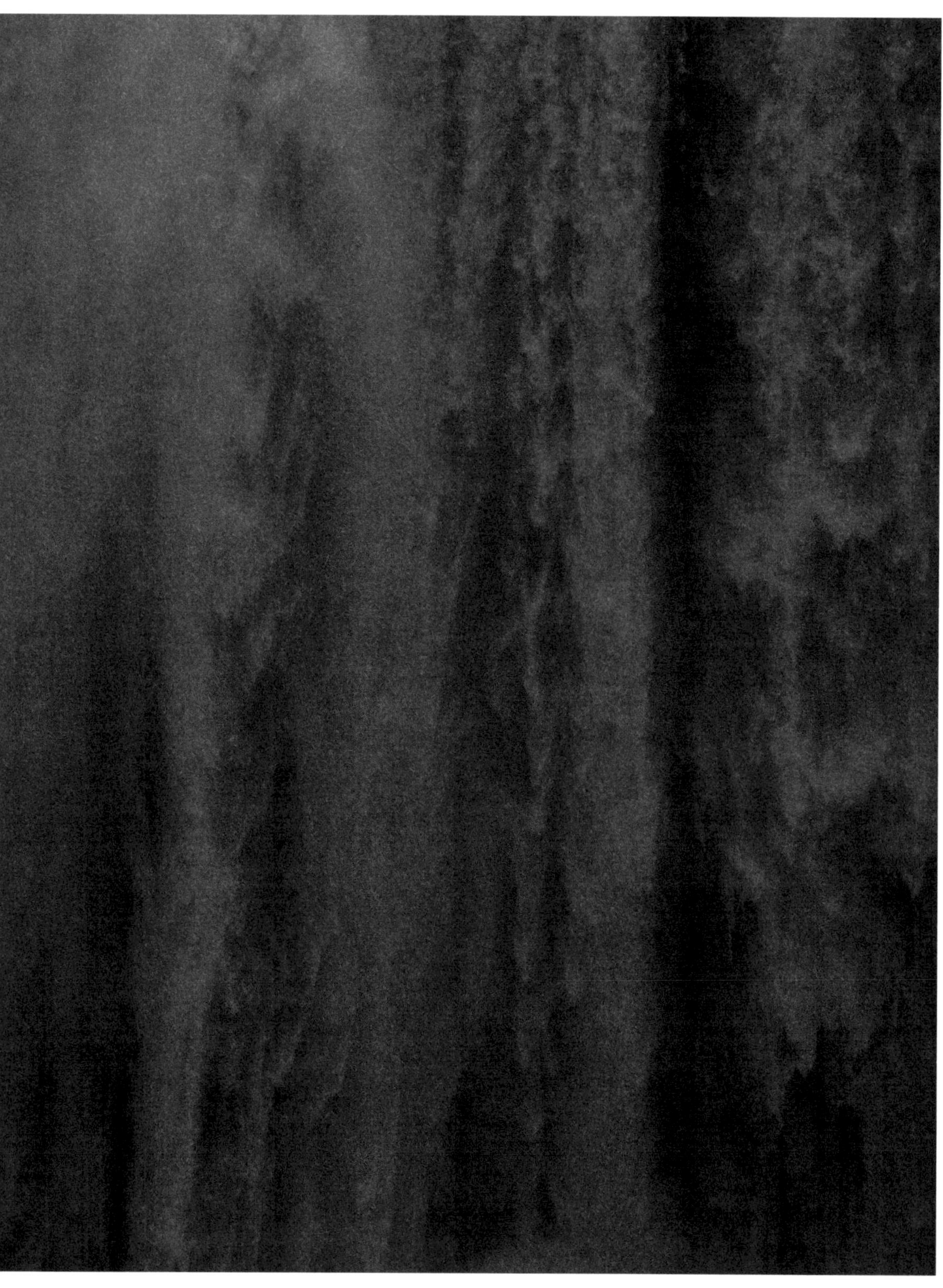

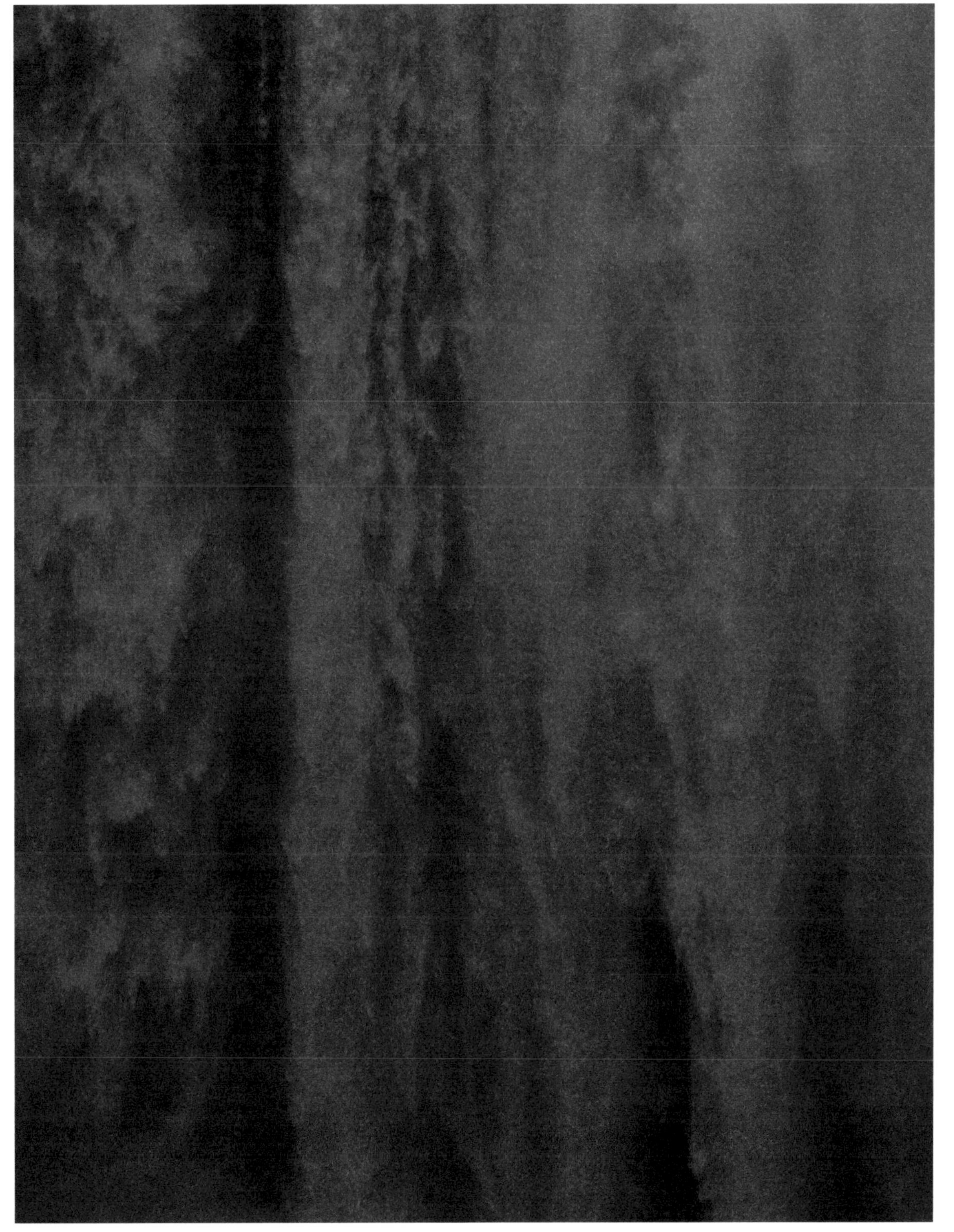

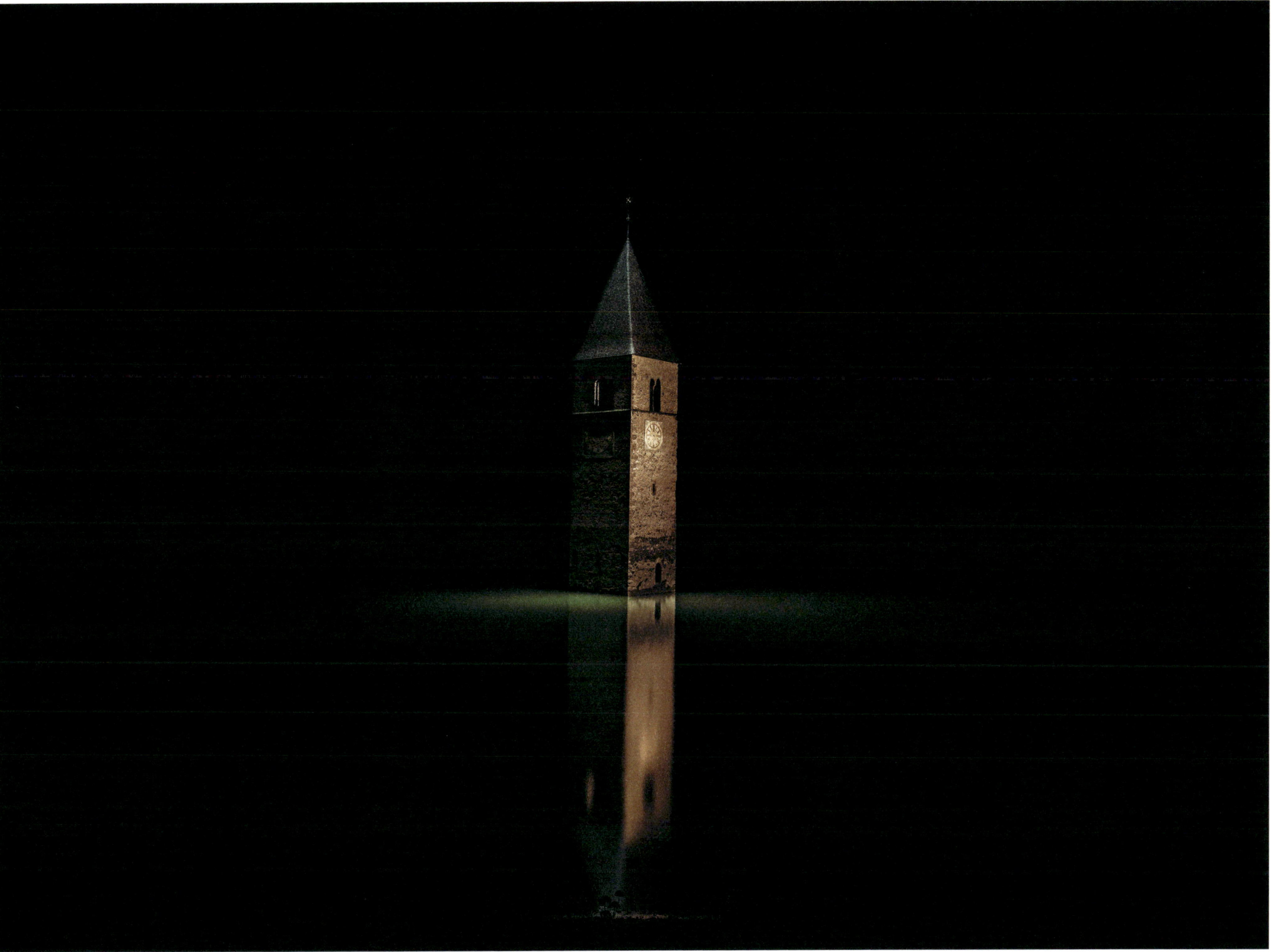

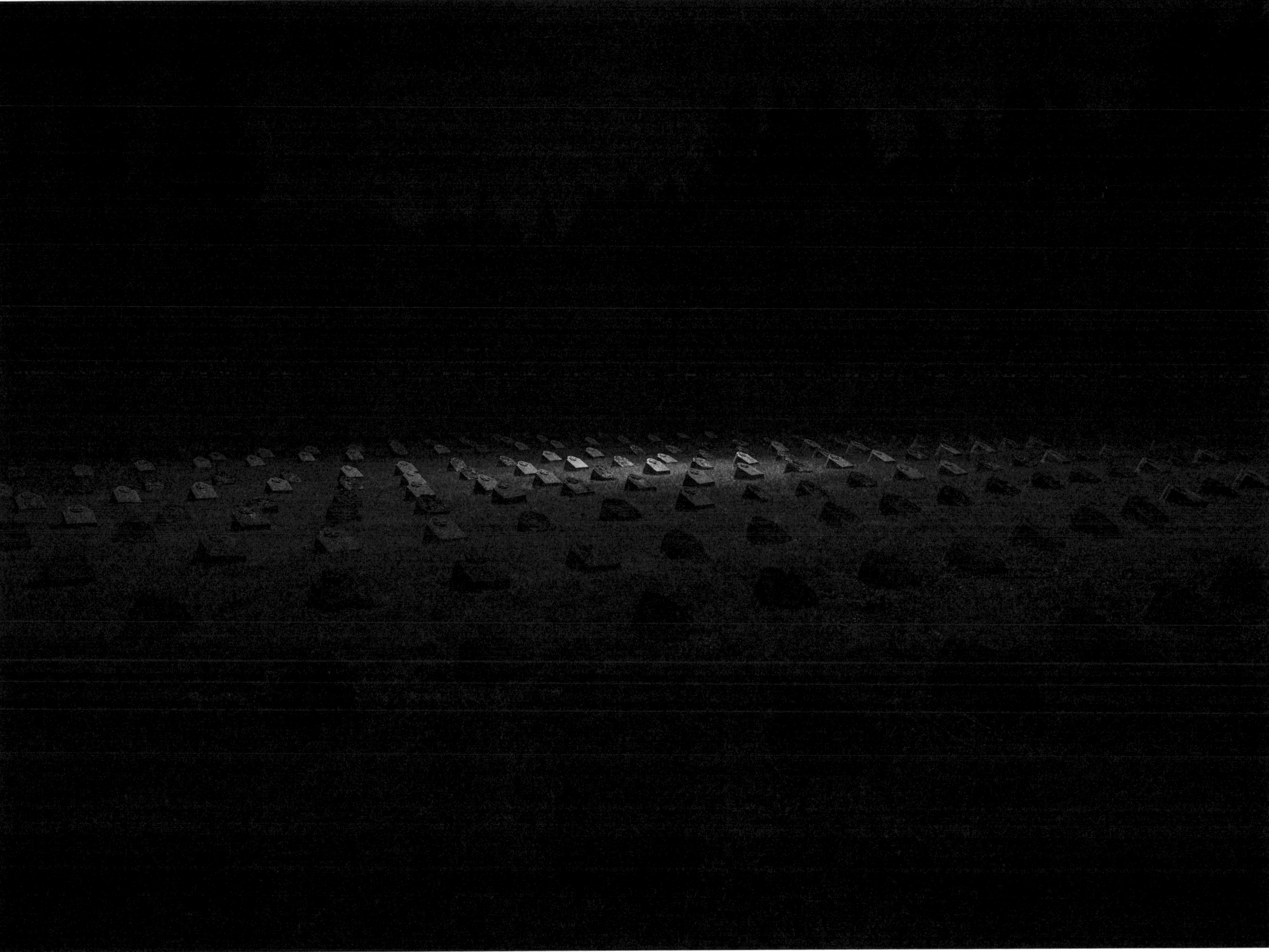

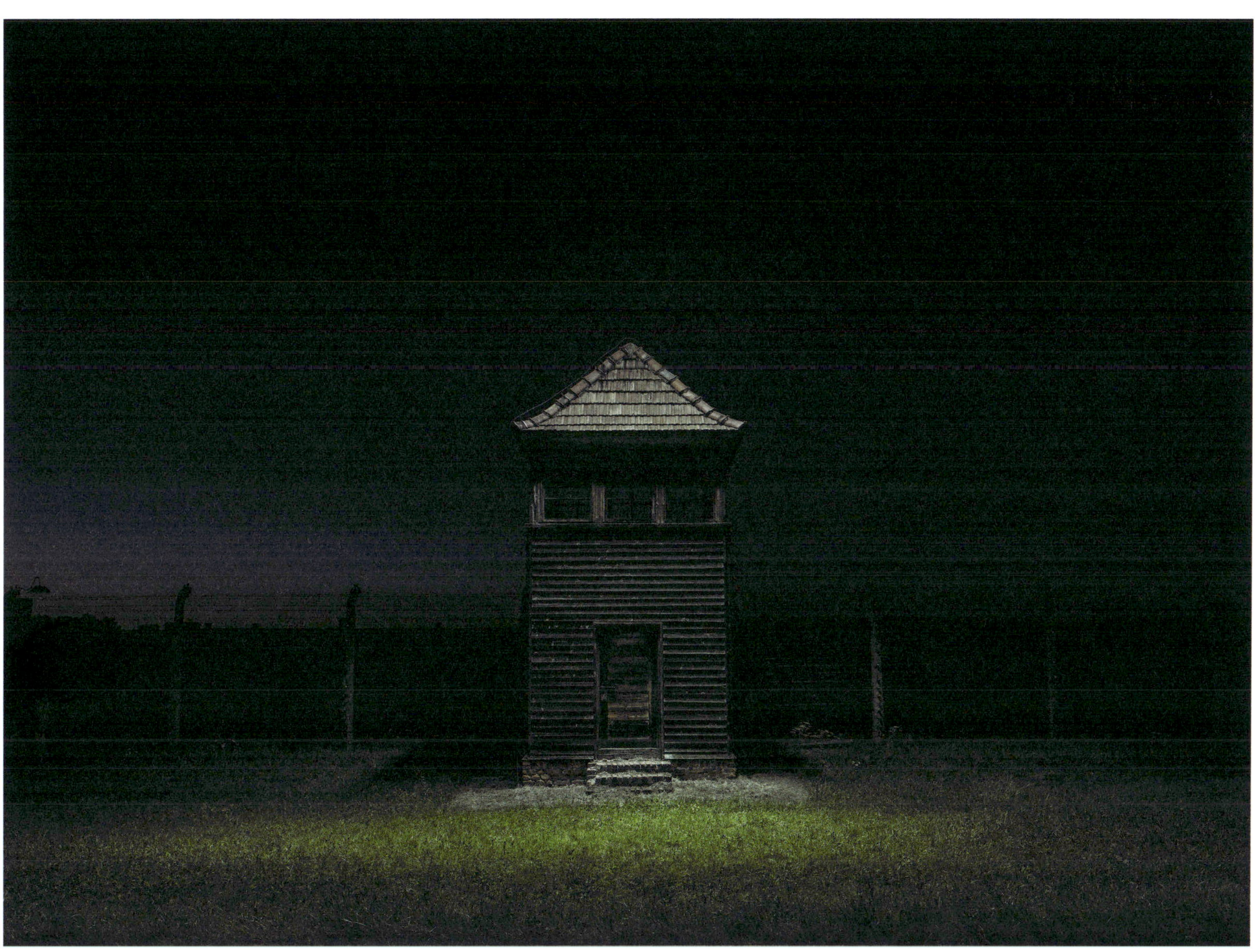

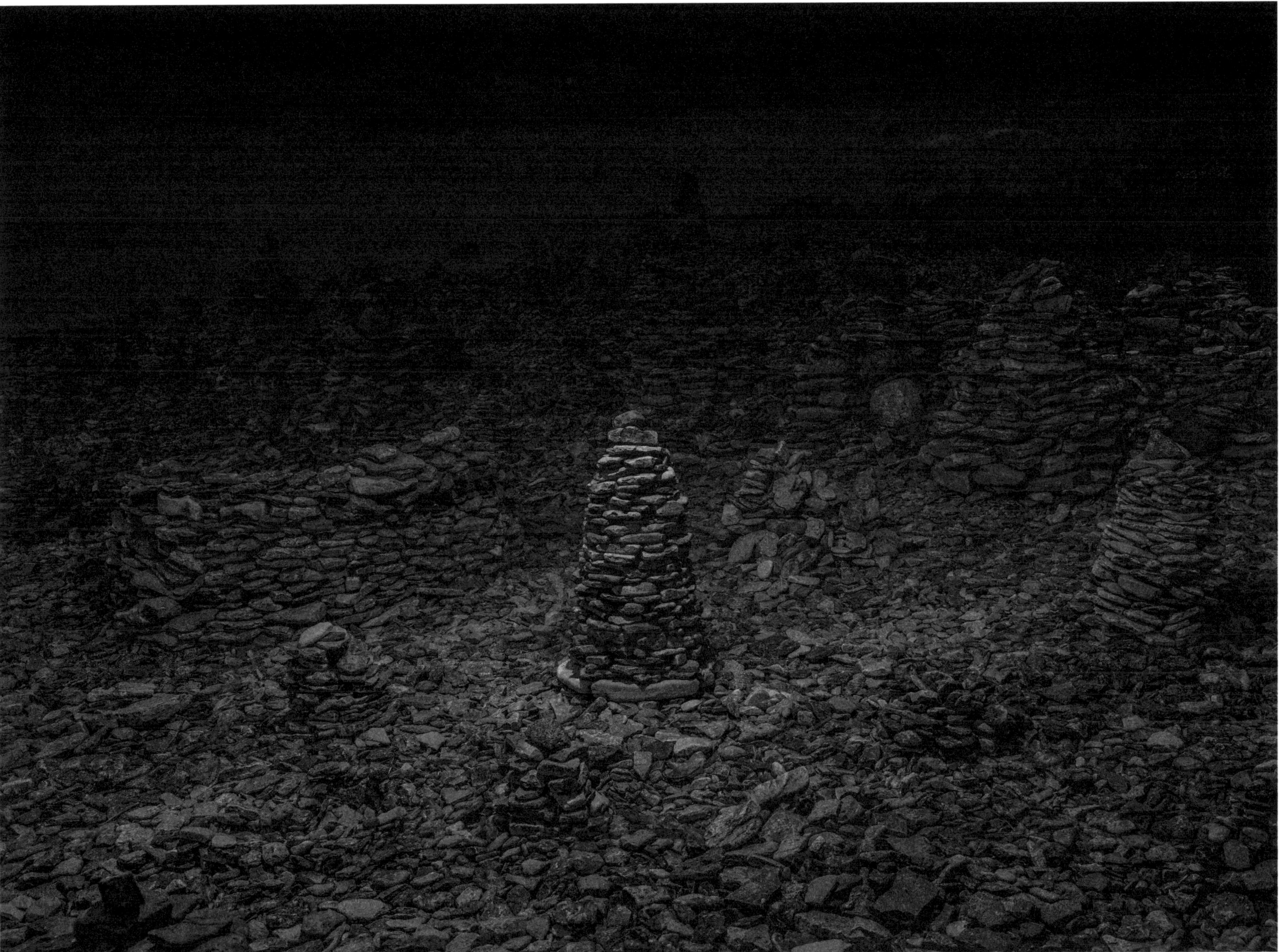

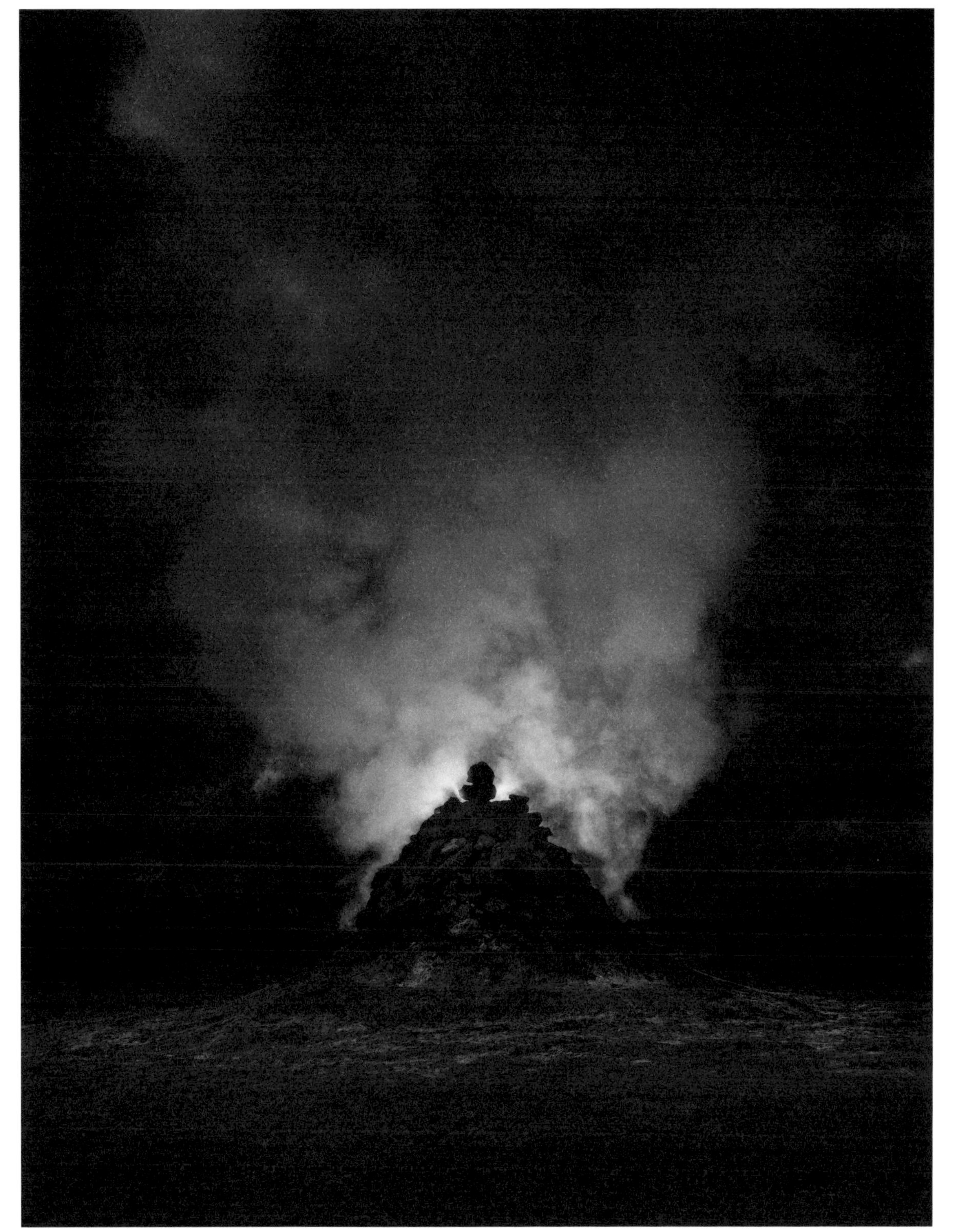

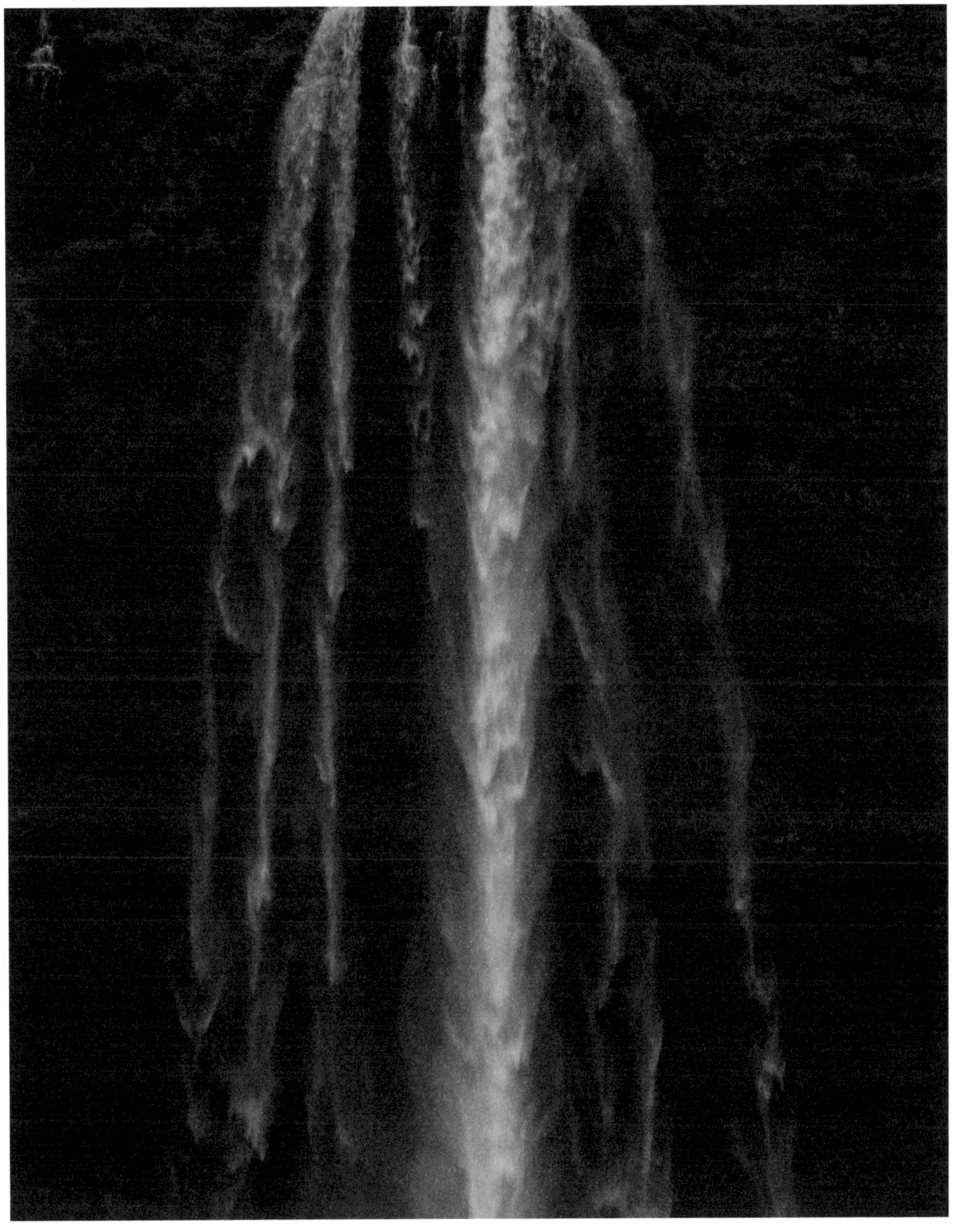

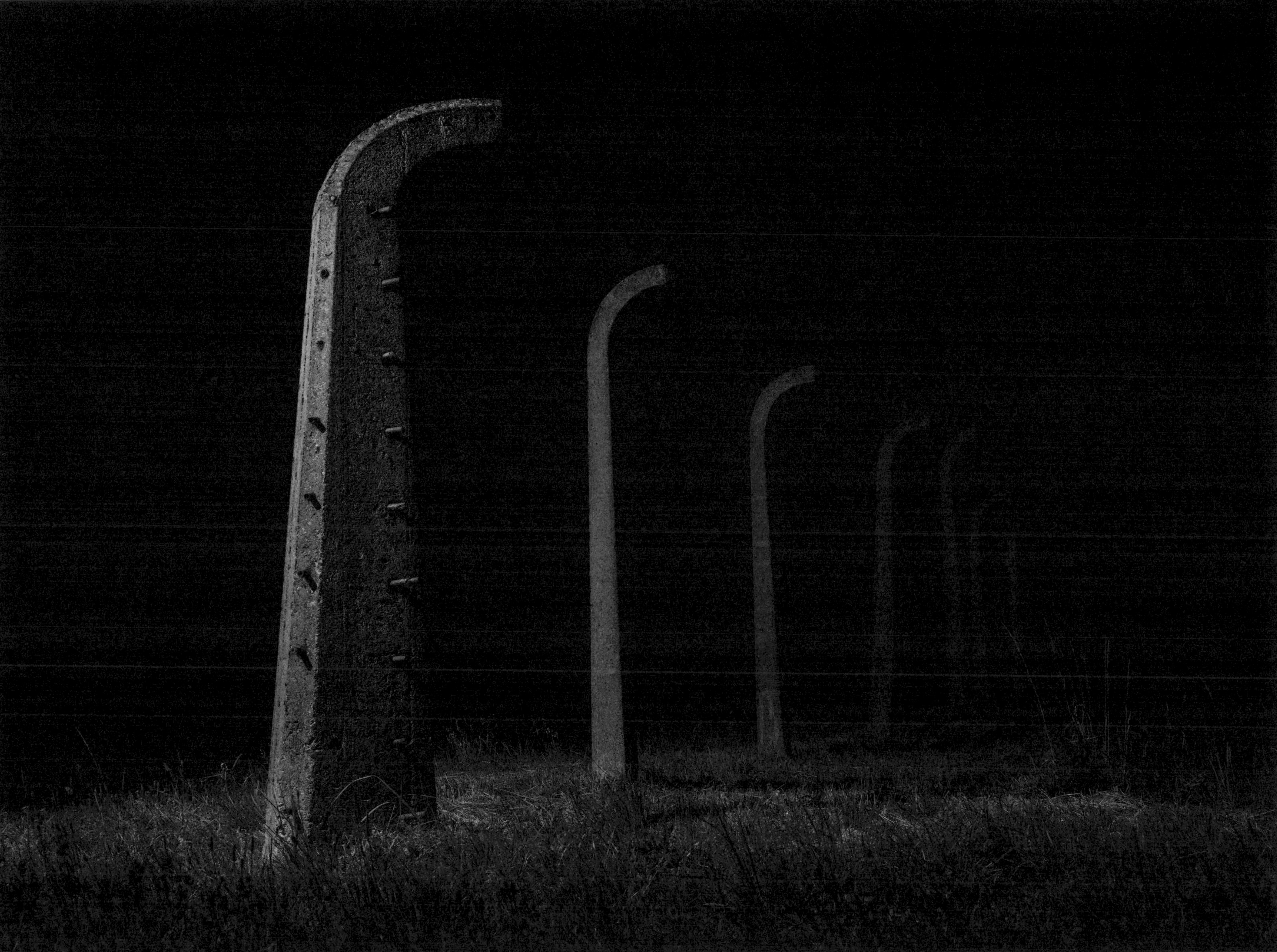

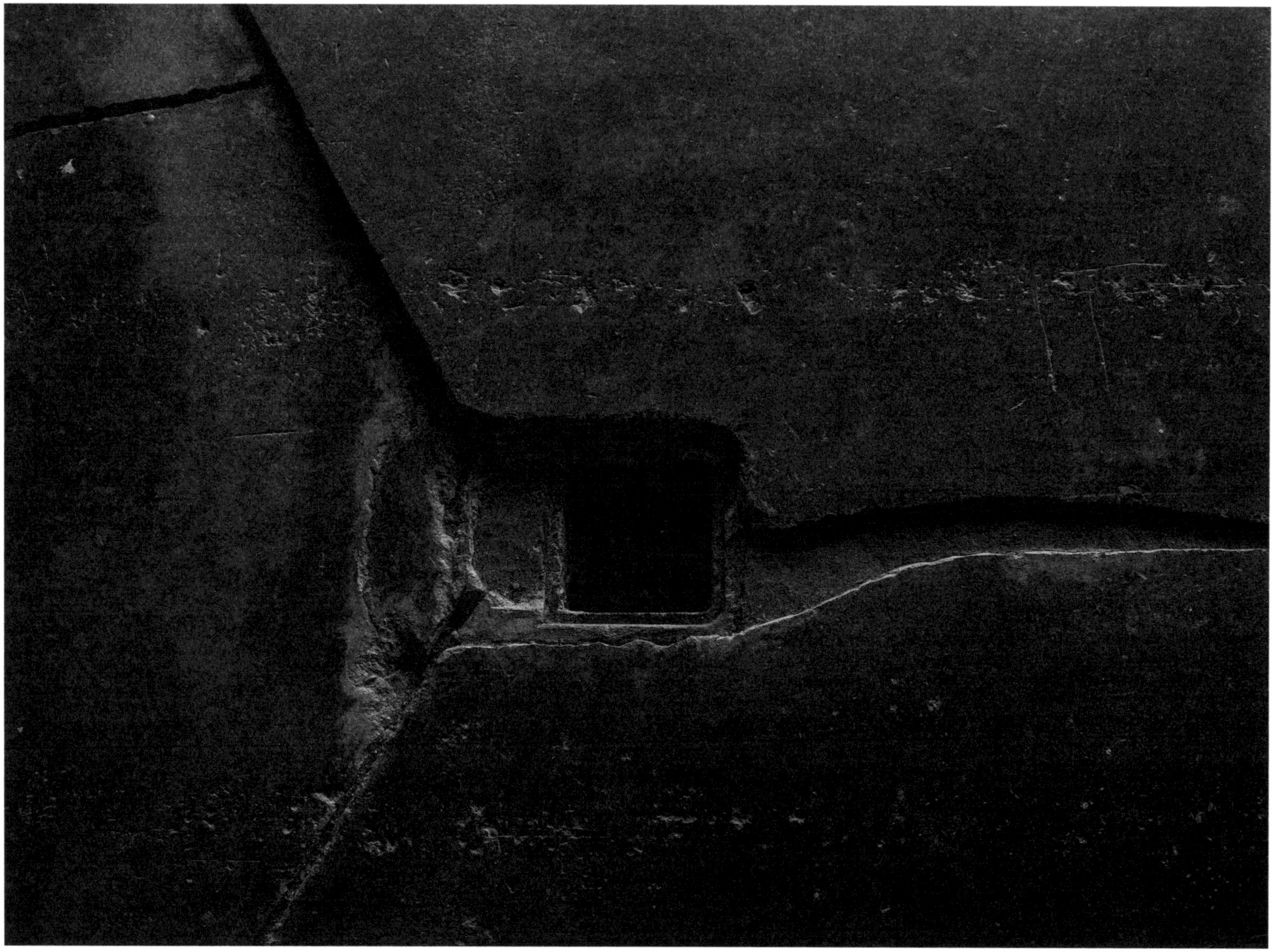

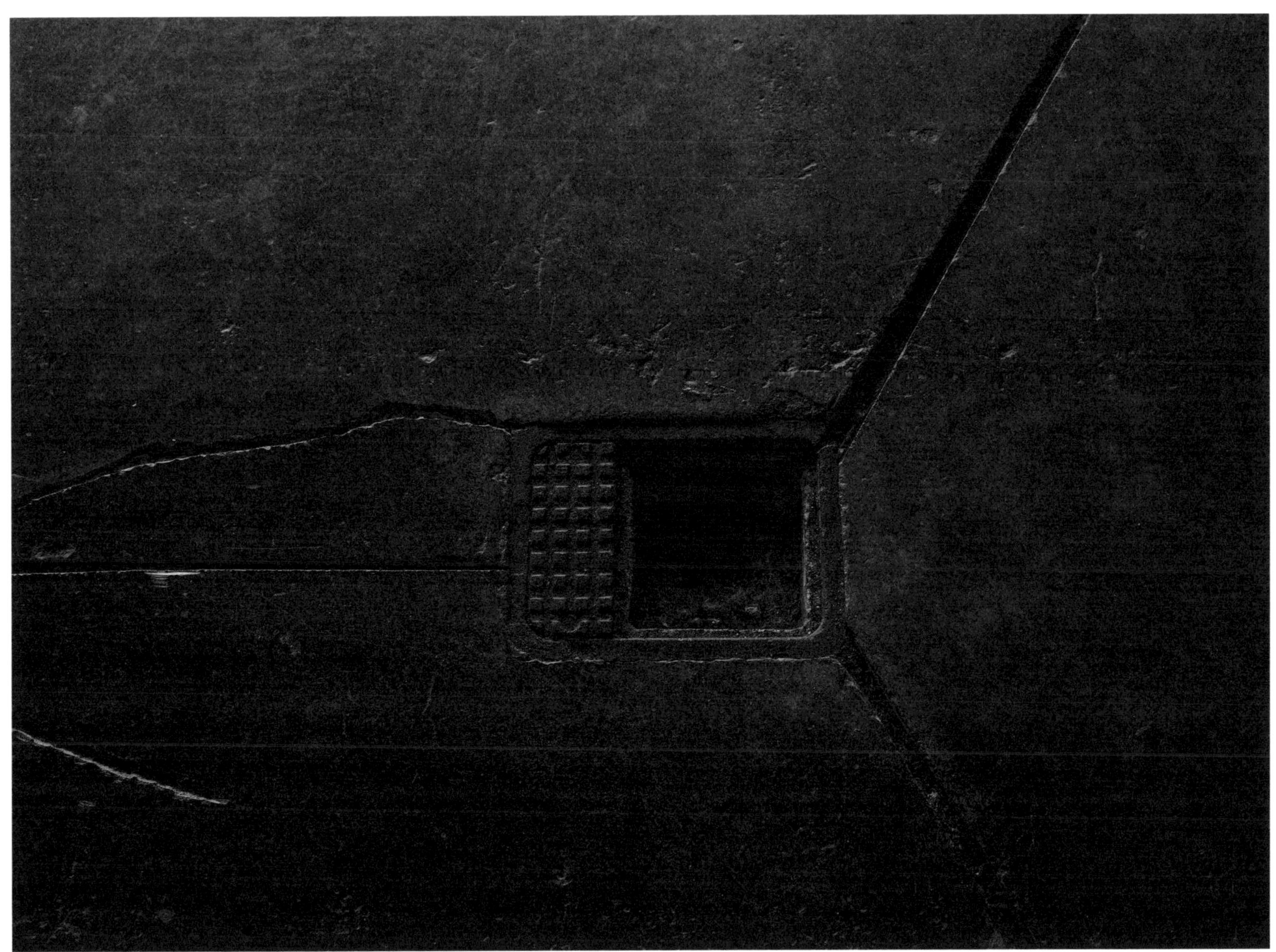

IV

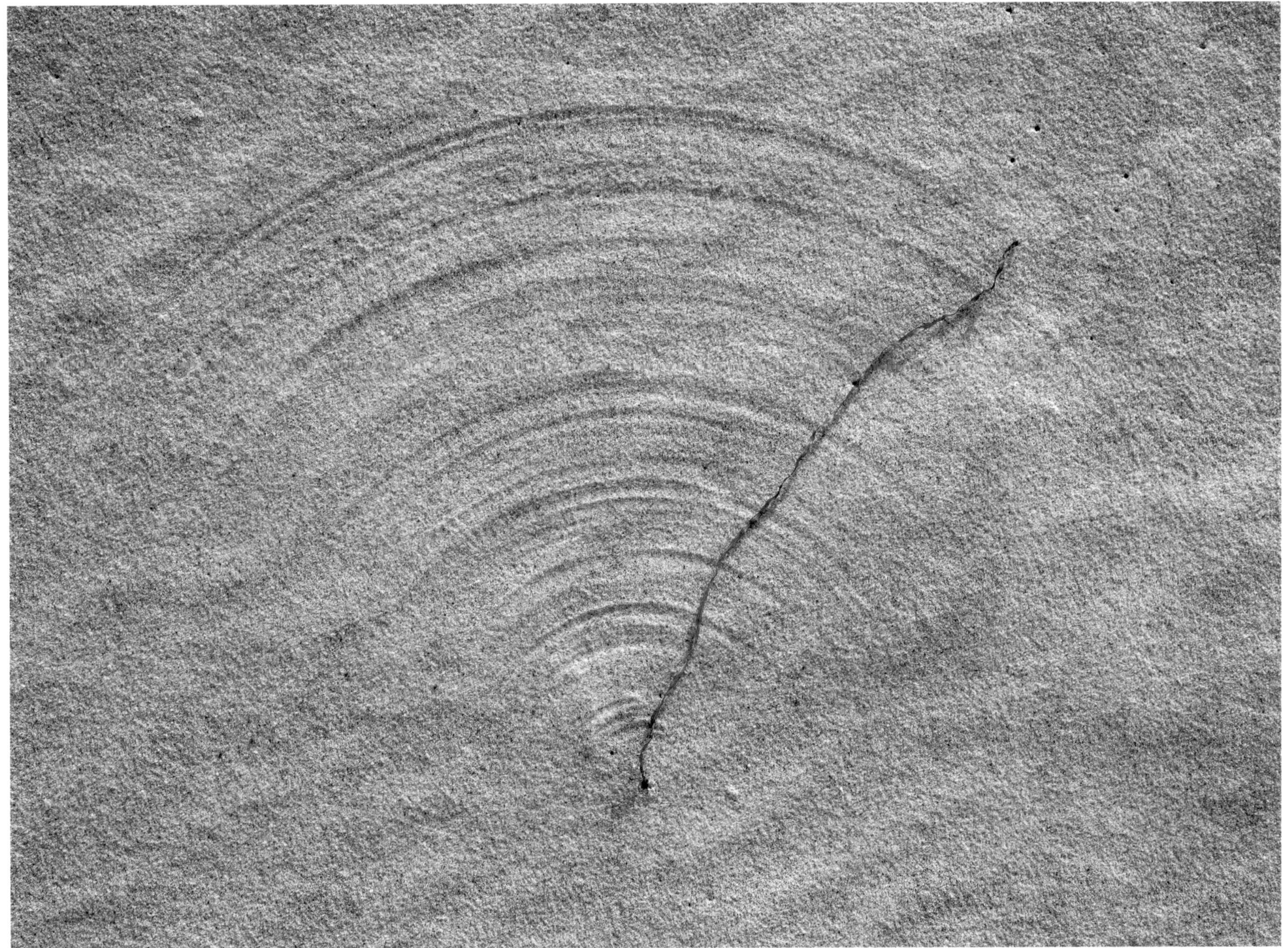

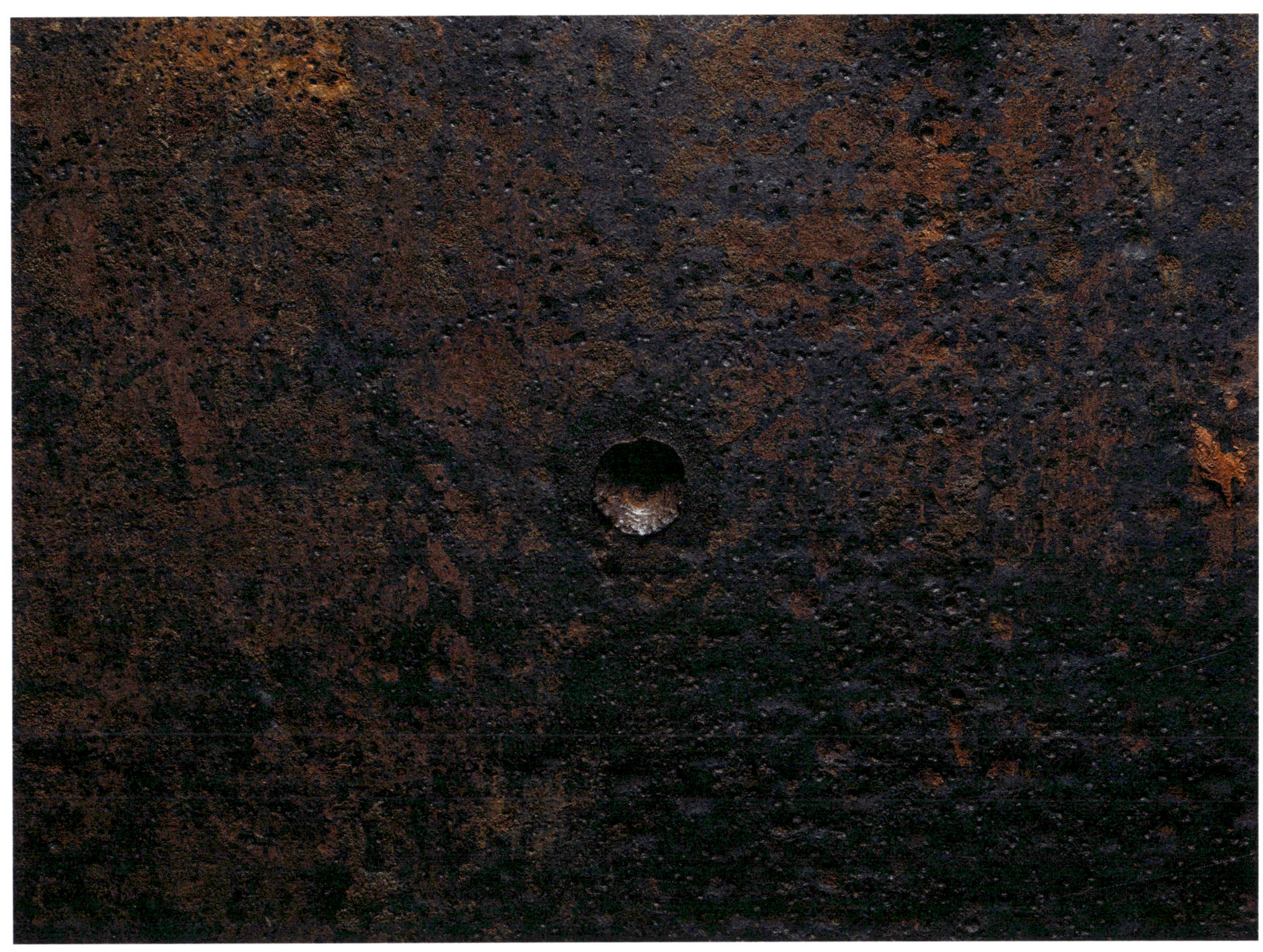

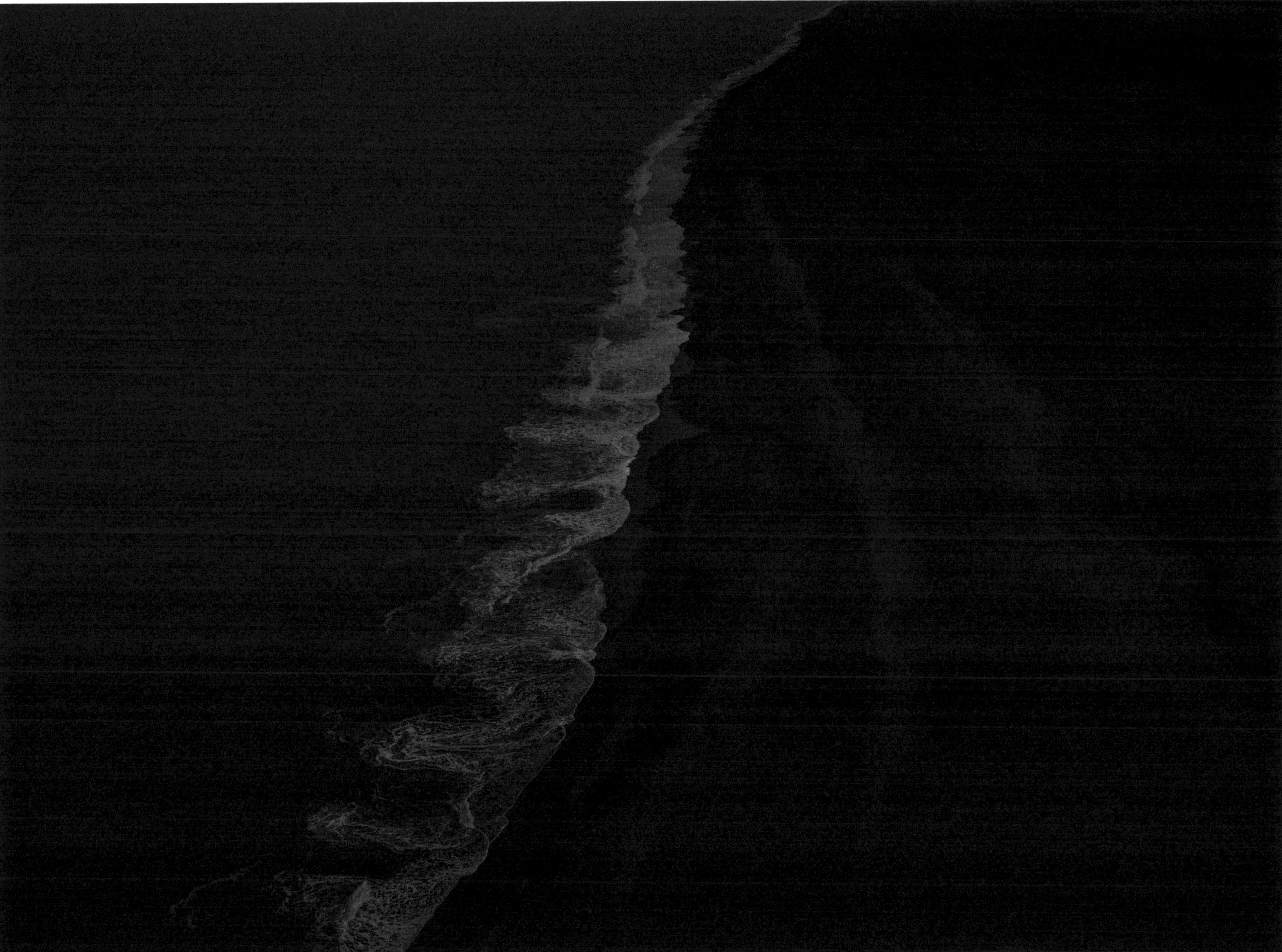

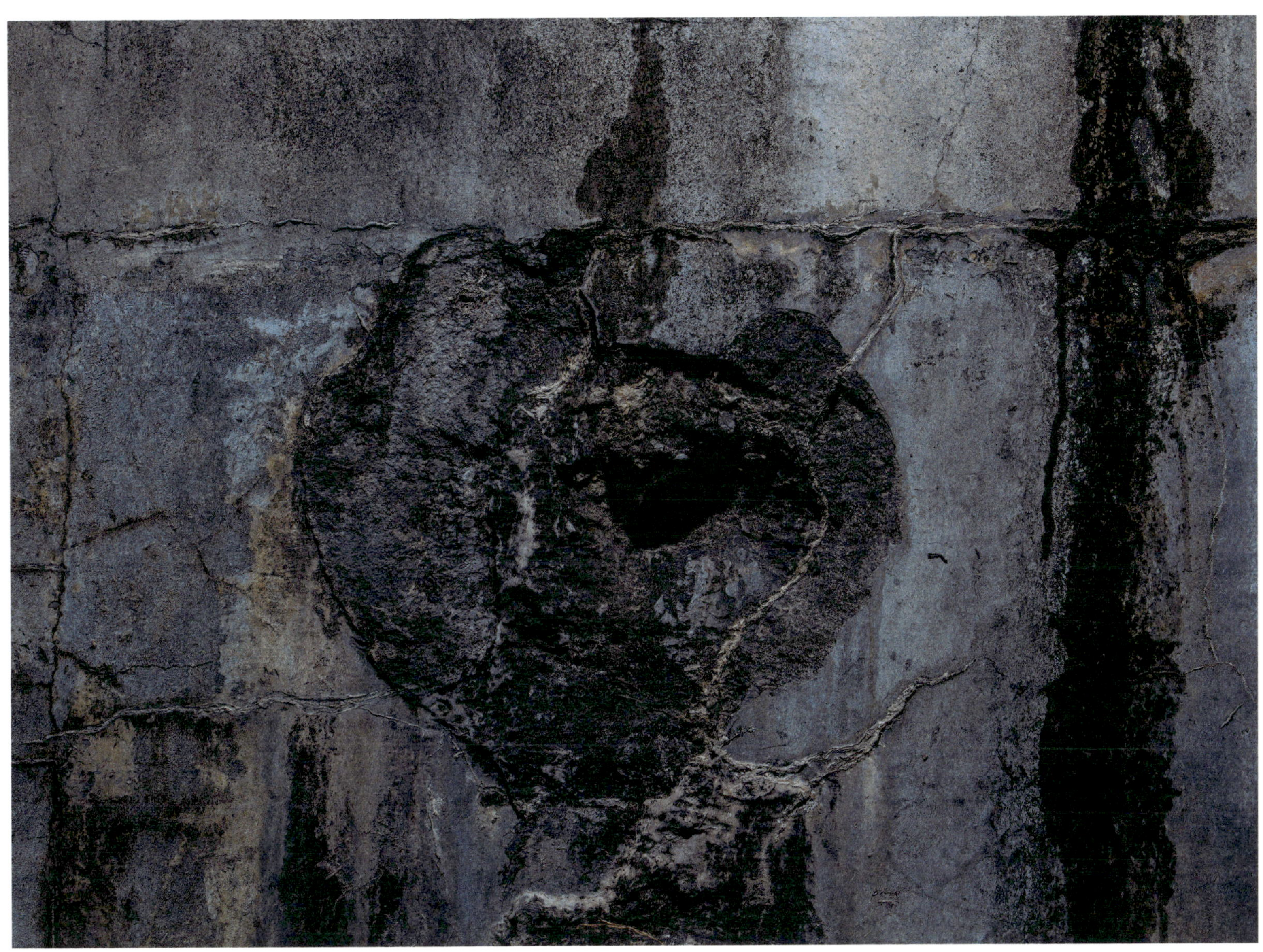

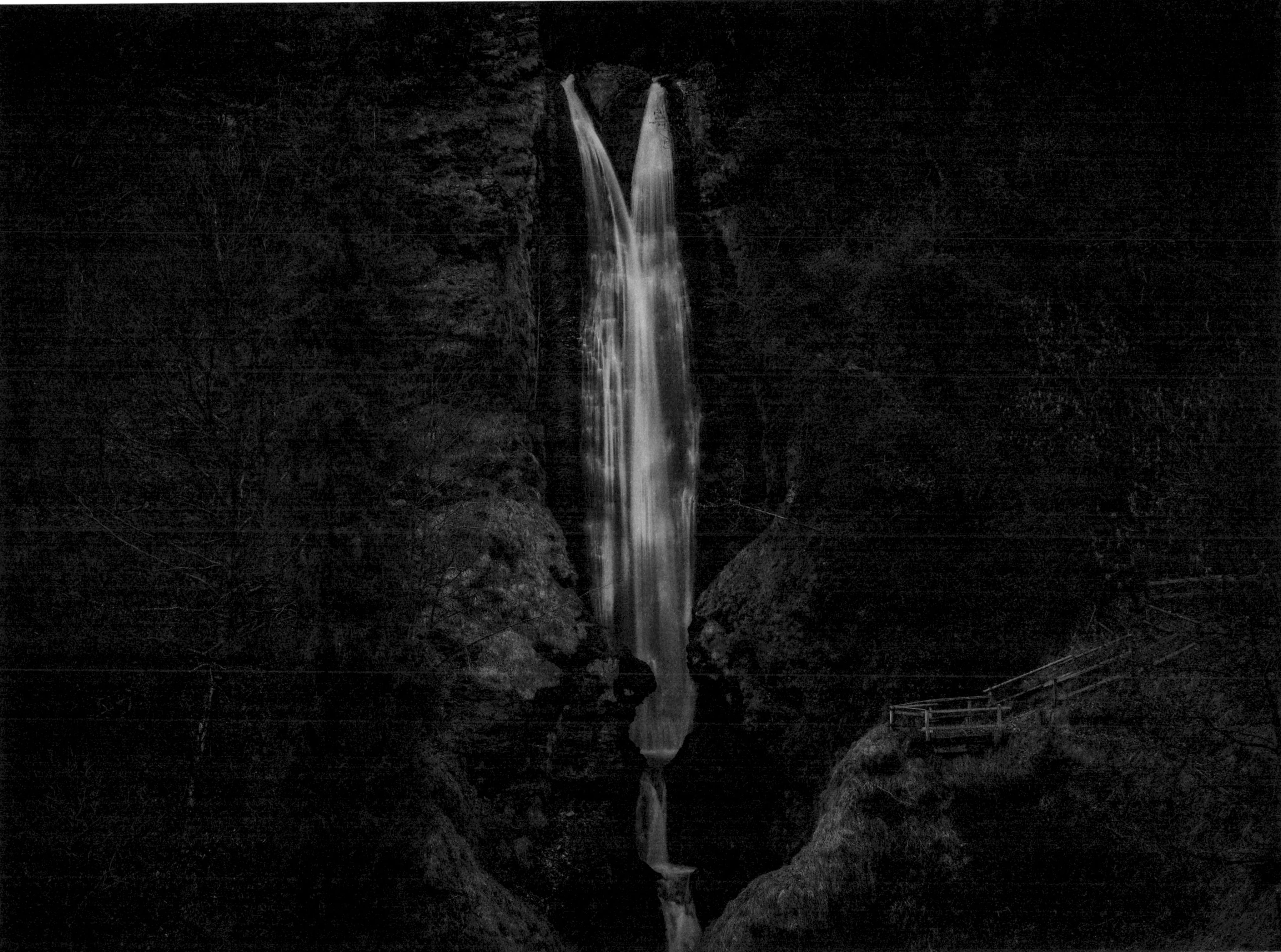

ACKNOWLEDGMENTS


I would like to thank Aalto University School of Arts, Design and Architecture,
Niko Luoma, Jyrki Parantainen, Jaakko Kahilaniemi, Ari Lahti, Nadine Barth,
Sonja Altmeppen, Franziska Lang, Arja Karhumaa, Mark Gisbourne and
Asia Zak Persons for all the help. Eeva, friends and family for being there.
And special thanks to Timothy Persons, Laura García Moreno-Torres, Katharina Peter,
Hannah Glauner at Gallery Taik Persons for providing invaluable support during the project.

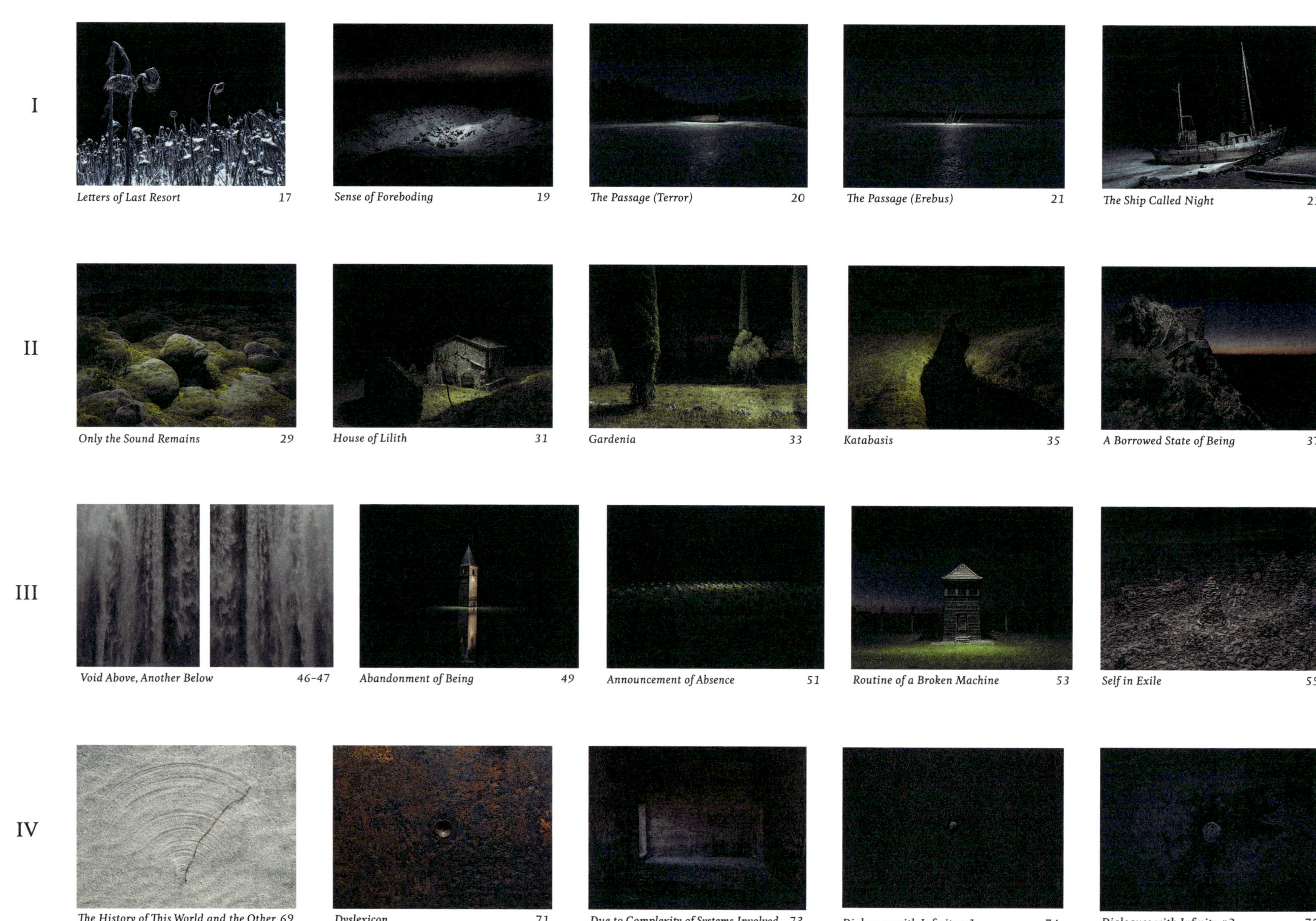

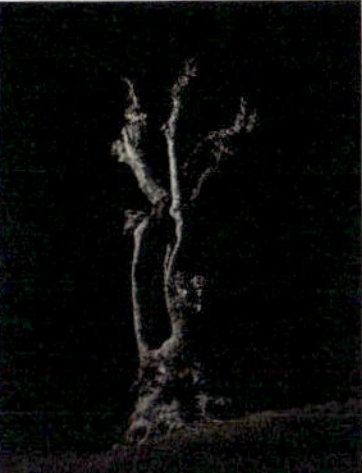



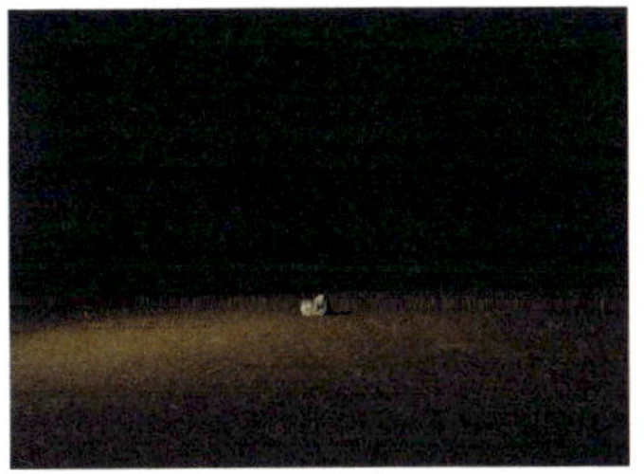

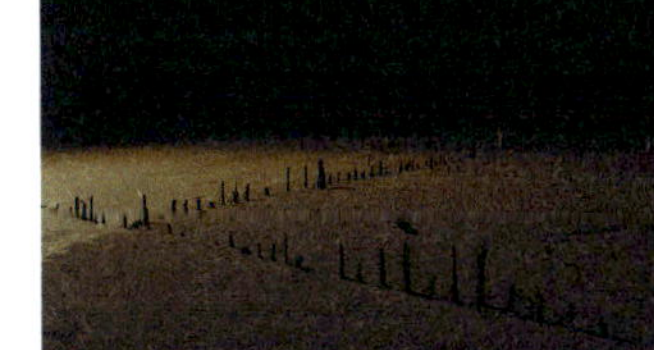

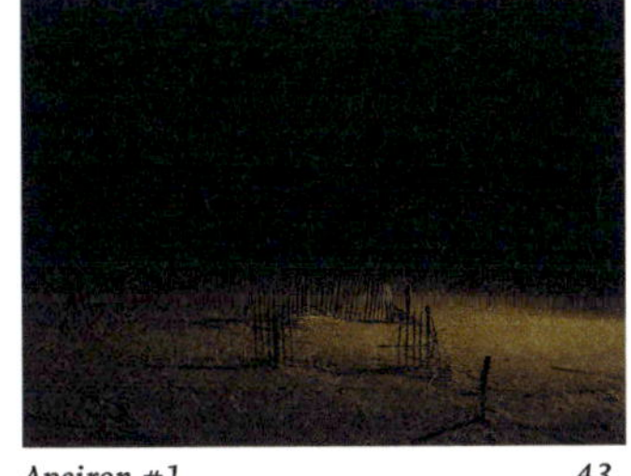

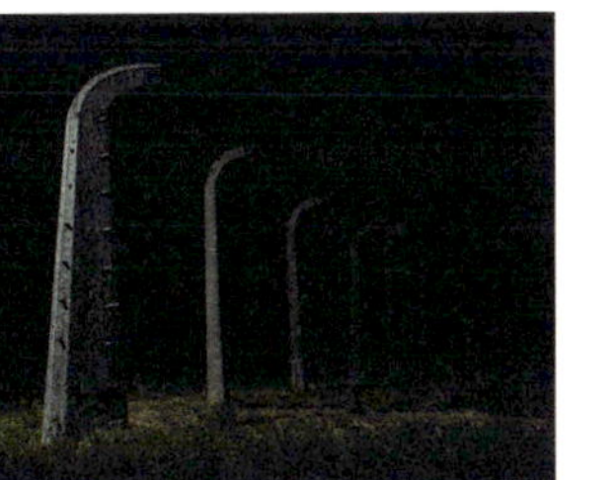

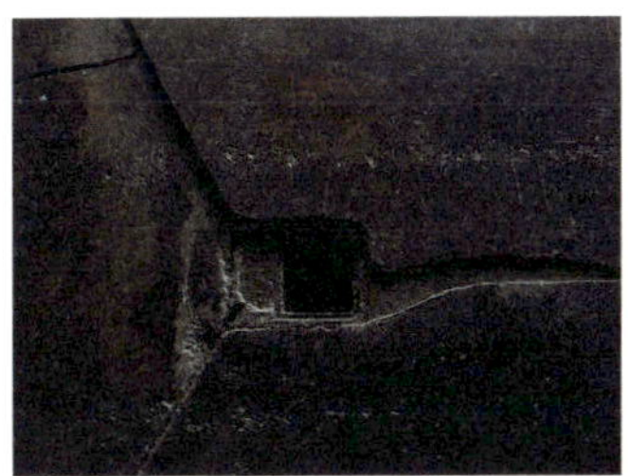

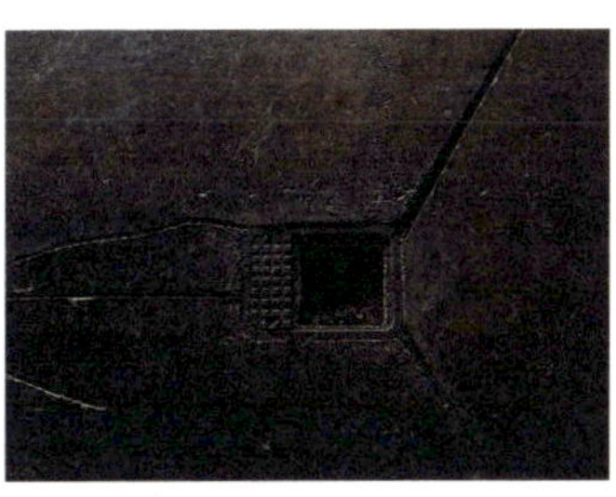

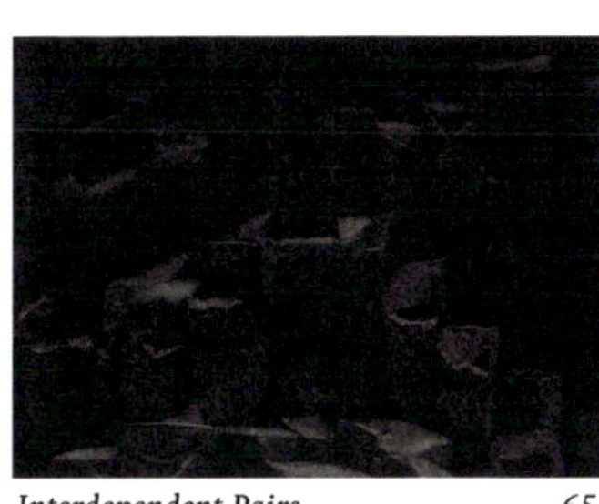



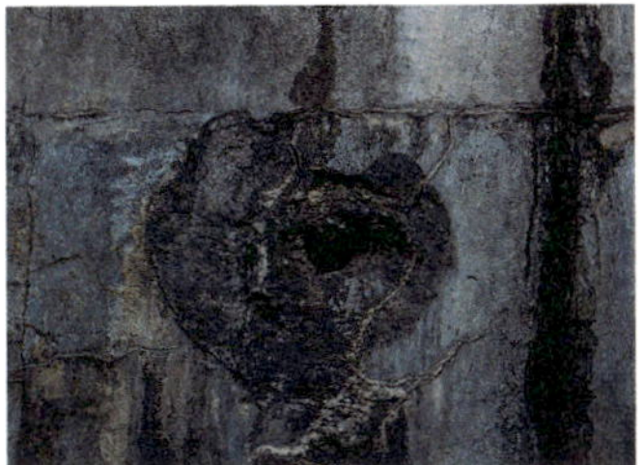

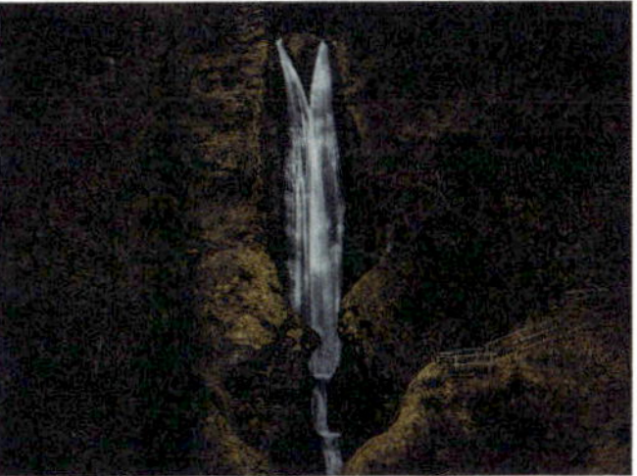

Editors:
Jyrki Parantainen, Petri Juntunen

Foreword:
Timothy Persons, Adjunct Professor at Aalto University, School of
Arts, Design and Architecture

Text:
Mark Gisbourne, Curator, Art Historian and Critic

Project management:
Sonja Altmeppen, Hatje Cantz

Copyediting:
John Wheelwright

Graphic design and typesetting:
Arja Karhumaa

Typeface:
Feijoa

Production:
Franziska Lang, Hatje Cantz

Reproductions:
Jan Scheffler, prints professional

Printind and binding:
DZA Druckerei zu Altenburg GmbH, Altenburg

Paper:
Lessebo smooth natural, 150 g/m²



Published by
Hatje Cantz Verlag GmbH
Mommsenstraße 27
10629 Berlin
Tel. +49 30 3464678-00
Fax +49 30 3464678-29
www.hatjecantz.de
A Ganske Publishing Group Company

Hatje Cantz books are available internationally at selected bookstores.
For more information about our distribution partners, please visit
our website at www.hatjecantz.com.

ISBN 978-3-7757-4355-6

Printed in Germany

Cover illustration
*The Ship Called Night*

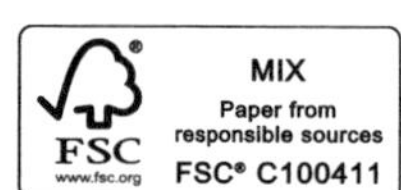